19.99

hotel
interior structures

WILEY-ACADEMY

Acknowledgements

I would like to thank all those hotels, hotel managers and staff, who have extended their accommodation, patience and support by allowing me to poke around rooms with camera, tripod and notebooks at all hours, most notably the Four Seasons, New York; the Four Seasons, Las Vegas; the Paris Hotel and Casino, Las Vegas; the Bellagio Hotel and Casino, Las Vegas; the Mandalay Bay, Las Vegas; the Morrisson, Dublin; the Albergo, Beirut; the Miramar and Dwar-el-Omda, Egypt; the Meridien Lingotto, Turin.

In addition to the hotels themselves, I would also like to thank hoteliers and designers who gave me time and attention for interviews, in particular Michael Graves, Gordon Campbell Grey, Charles Gruwell and Ian Schrager.

I would also like to acknowledge all those in the many press offices around the world who have assembled, posted, re-assembled and re-posted as per my request information and images on hotels, and arranged appointments and interviews.

On a more personal note, I want to express my thanks to Lennox Lodge for tolerating work-in-progress; to my editor, Maggie Toy, for extended patience; and to Mariangela Palazzi-Williams for her dedication in bringing the manuscript to publication.

Photographic Credits

One Aldwych photos courtesy of the hotel; The Metropolitan Hotel photos courtesy of the hotel; SoHo Grand photos courtesy of Nancy J Felldman Associates; Grand Hyatt Berlin photos courtesy of the hotel; Hotel Montalembert photos courtesy of the hotel; Hotel Albergo photos © Eleanor Curtis and pp. 64, 65 (bottom right), 65 (top left), 69 (right) coutesy of the hotel; Mercer Hotel photos © Simon Watson Photos courtesy of the hotel; Halkin photos courtesy of the hotel; Morgans, Royalton, Paramount, Delano and Mondrian photos courtesy of Dan Klores and Associates; St Martins' Lane photos © Todd Berle and courtesy of Dan Klores and Associates; W New York, W Atlanta, W San Francisco and W Seattle photos courtesy of GCI Group; The Standard photos © Todd Berle and courtesy of the hotel; Morrison photos © Eleanor Curtis; Dwar El Omda photos © Marc Balley; Four Seasons Istanbul photos courtesy of Columbus Communications; Four Seasons Milano photos courtesy of the hotel; Le Meridien Lingotto photos © Eleanor Curtis and pp. 169, 173 (bottom), 177 © Gianno Gardia; Paris Las Vegas photos © Eleanor Curtis; Bellagio Las Vegas photos © Eleanor Curtis and pp. 191 (bottom), 193, 194, 196 (top) © Russel MacMasters and courtesy of the hotel; Mandalay Bay Las Vegas photos © Eleanor Curtis and pp. 199, 200, 202, 203 courtesy of hotel; Four Seasons Las Vegas photos © Eleanor Curtis and pp. 208, 209 (bottom) © Mary Nicols and courtesy of the hotel; Sheraton Miramar photos © Eleanor Curtis; Park Hyatt Tokyo photos courtesy of the hotel; Hyatt Regency Fukuoka photos courtesy of Michael Graves Architects; Hyatt Regency Paris photos courtesy of Murphy Jahn Architects; Sheraton Paris Airport photos © Delde Von Schsewen and courtesy of the hotel; Four Seasons New York photos © Eleanor Curtis and pp. 251, 254 (top), 257 (bottom & top) courtesy of hotel; Four Seasons Canary Wharf photos courtesy of United Designers.

Published by
WILEY-ACADEMY

A division of
JOHN WILEY & SONS
Baffins Lane
Chichester
West Sussex PO19 1UD

ISBN: 0–470–85740–4

First published in paperback 2003

Other Wiley Editorial Offices
New York • Weinheim • Brisbane • Singapore • Toronto

Cover design by Artmedia Press, London

Typeset and designed by Florence Production, Stoodleigh, Devon
Printed and bound in Italy

CONTENTS

PREFACE

This volume attempts to draw out some current trends in hotel interior design that have emerged within the last 10 years.

The projects presented here are representative of particular styles and approaches to hotel interior design, and its coverage herein is exclusively that of interiors, and not of exteriors.

I am reluctant to make explicit the criteria for selection for fear of oversimplification, and am aware of the danger of tagging projects with labels that may divert the reader from other more delicate design themes that the designer has worked painstakingly on. In the attempt to redress this balance I have tried to show as many angles of the interiors as possible, to enable the reader to view the design details for himself.

However, it has been necessary to group the projects according to some commonalities and allow the most dominant themes to surface. The projects presented here form groupings of styles, based on common themes, that were chosen for having qualities that resonate within the wider discipline of interior design and that make important contributions to the growing market of hotel business – namely, giving hotels a strong and marketable design identity.

The selection has been made from a choice of completed projects and was constrained by the availability of images and documentation; as a result, there are many new and exciting projects that are not included here.

There are also many more hotel projects that I would like to have detailed but which were simply too far afield to document adequately and within my limited time frame. For example, the new hotels of Morocco and India that are exquisite in detail and a wonder of colours, as well as being of interest in their own right, also hold relevance as design reference.

In addition, the projects presented are more heavily weighted towards Europe and the USA than the Near, Middle and Far East, Africa and Australasia. This is not deliberate but a result of my being based on the European side of the world, with limited time and resources.

That said, this volume hopes to give hotel owners, hotel designers and those working in the wider field of interior design, a valuable insight into the what, why and how of current design trends across a few stretches of the globe.

INTRODUCTION

The 21st century guest and the new hotel

Who are the hotel guests of today and what do they do in hotels? What are their expectations of a hotel and how can design address these different needs, tastes and desires?

Style and service, comfort and luxury, personal and authentic, creative and intriguing. All these and more are what the modern guest demands from a hotel, or so it seems . . .

Today's hotel brochures advertising the more recently designed hotels play on the theme of 'the modern or urban lifestyle' or on meeting the needs of the 'new jet set of the information age'. Nowhere written is there an exact profile of this info-laden jet set of the 21st century (read guest), nor is there a complete checklist of things this guest likes to do. In turn, nowhere is there a complete checklist of essential design components for hotel interiors, for each project has its own brief (consider new hotel versus renovation versus adaptation) and each designer comes with his or her speciality (consider architecture, furniture, fashion or textiles).

For want of a definition, the new concepts surrounding globalisation that are associated with our 'modern worlds' will be used here as the lens with which to focus on hotel interior design.

First, some labels; then our 'modern worlds; and finally, the hotels and their spaces.

Sticky labels

Many labels have been used in the last two decades to describe the types of hotel that have shifted their attention from function-based to interior architecture and design. After the boom of business hotels came the 'boutique' hotel in the early 1980s (attention to small details), the atrium hotel (vast post-modern architecture), the designer hotel (designed by a known name) and, at the other end of the scale, the resort hotel (Vegas, Disney, etc.). Today, we have 'urban resorts' that aim to match the essence of urban living with personal lifestyle, answering the call of the new generation of modern globe-trotters.

There are many more types in between and outside of these labels, and this proliferation of variety in hotel design and hotel identity acts as a testimony to the recent and rapid growth within this design and business sector.

Crudely put, some of the reasons for this growth lie in today's ever expanding possibilities afforded by easy travel, globalisation and wider knowledge access, and an increase in disposable income. And not only have these market forces pushed for a better quality of hotel with a fresh face on design, but they have also welcomed fresh blood into the business – a new breed of hotel entrepreneur and his creative team of hybrid designers (see Talks).

These 'push and pull' aspects to the business – the modern 'global' life of the guest and the fresh approach to hotel design philosophy that have revamped an otherwise conservative industry – are fuelling an exciting and competitive period in hotel interior design.

Modern worlds

Places

Are hotels simply places to rest our heads for a night or two, or are they more than this? Are they places instead where we desire to be someone other than who we are, places for fantasy, places to dream? Or, on a more mundane level, is a hotel merely another place of work?

Guests want designs that will complement these needs to one extent or another; and of fundamental importance to this is the reason for our stay at the hotel.

Stereotypically, business trips are quick-paced and demand a hotel that will support fast turn around and provide efficiency, technology, reliable and quick restaurants and bars, and, of course, peace and quiet. City breaks are typically spread over a long weekend and demand a little more from the hotel, that it acts as a microcosm of the city visited, and a place instantiating local culture: the guest wants to experience a slice of the city within the four walls of the hotel. Airport stay-overs are brief but demand that the hotel act as a 24 hour service centre with high priorities on easy access to international communications and information. Lastly, there are holidays, where a clean break from the daily routine of life back home is expected, in one way or another. The resort hotel can do this by offering 'another world' (usually of entertainment) for pure escapism, or by offering another level of life where the guest may 'live' like royalty for a week or two.

Blurring edges

Aside from the last category of holiday resort hotels, functional distinctions between the others are becoming more and more blurred. This blurring has been afforded by the increasingly global nature of modern life; on the one side it encourages guests to demand a mix of services that allows a more enriched 'experience' of the hotel, and on the other, it encourages the hotel to offer a fusion of functions.

For example, the business traveller may have access to book hotels via the internet and may also have the opportunity to carry on business from his room in one of many hotels rather than just 'business hotels'. The city stomper may also choose to surf the internet in search of the most interesting-looking hotel with a selection of digital images to help his choice, rather than using the travel agent. The one-night city stop-over between flights may also have more choice with the seamless travelling afforded by new 'speedlink' trains between airport and city.

In contrast resort hotels must compete with the improved and impressive multi-media based exposure of other worlds – computer simulations, high quality still image reproduction, and film – and offer something that will exceed well-informed expectations. Thus, the architecture and interiors must take themes to the edge of fantasy and offer an experience like no other. Vegas 'entertainment architecture' is a case in point.

Our 21st-century guest needs a hotel that encompasses modern design on a creative, interesting, stimulating and intelligent level that will appeal to him in both the global (in touch with the world) and the personal (in touch with him) sense.

The hotel designer, in turn, must move with these technology-changing times, and offer a better 'experience' of hotel that can match more specifically these individual needs and tastes, rather than that of a stereotype. And over the last two decades, hotel design has moved.

The hotels

A back drop

The idea of the 'boutique' hotel was born in the early 1980s from an experimental idea by hotel entrepreneur Ian Schrager. Teaming up with interior designer Andrée Putman, Morgans Hotel of New York was the first hotel to emphasise the experience of hotel design from the inside. This was a turning point in the approach to hotel design and we have since seen this 'boutique' idea transform itself into a 'hip' hotel, a 'designer' hotel, an 'urban resort' through to a place for 'visceral' experiences. These labels can be a little vague and also overlap in what they imply: but the new 'contemporary' hotels are all of this and more.

They are 'boutique' in the sense that they are on a smaller scale with attention to fine detail. They are also 'hip' in the sense that they play on fashion trends and attract a style-conscious guest. They are 'designer' hotels in the sense that they often have a designer's signature on the interiors. They are an 'urban resort' in that they offer a hide-out within the hub of the city and at the same time capture the essence of the city. And, more recently, they offer 'visceral' experiences through the creative use of colours, textures and sounds. But they are more than just the sum of these parts.

Perhaps the most important and subtle turning point in the development of interior design trends for the contemporary hotel was the introduction of the narrative into design, requiring that the designer view the project more as a film director, theatre set director, or author of fiction.

In these new projects the interior design of the hotel pushes the effects of design further, and carries the responsibility for the success of the overall theme from the large public scale of the lobby or restaurant, down to the detailed personal level in the bedrooms and bathrooms. It is the 'experience' of this overall theme or concept, expressed through the interiors, with which the guest will identify and will carry away as their memory of the hotel.

The spaces

Lobby

The lobby is one of the public spaces of hotels that has undergone a distinct transformation in terms of design over the last ten years. Whereas the first designed hotels deliberately played down the role of the lobby (see Morgans, New York), the more recent designs have used the lobby as the focal point for the hotel's design theme or design narrative.

The lobby has reclaimed its traditional role as a place for social activities and is now the place 'to be seen'. Heavy and explicit on design details (see work of Philippe Starck) including incredible works of art or sculptures (see One Aldwych, London or Bellagio, Las Vegas), the lobby has become a social hub not only for hotel guests but also with the local community of the particular city which it is situated in.

Often with lounge, bar and restaurants leading from the main lobby, the bulk of the hotel (rooms and services) can easily fade into the background. The lobby has become in some instances a stage set with theatrical lighting (see Paramount, New York), an organic garden (see W New York), a fashion cat-walk with permanent DJ (see Standard, LA), or a city film set (see Paris, Las Vegas).

City hotels that often design intimate, sometimes colourful lobby spaces, with exquisite furniture and tailor made lighting designs, demonstrate how important the lobby has become not only for spending time in (socialising, relaxing, meetings) but also as the grandest expression of the hotel's overall design theme. First impressions of the hotel are made on immediate entry through the lobby to the check-in and it is here that the design theme must communicate. Whether grand and classical, or hip and playful, or themed for entertainment, the lobby is the focal point of the hotel.

Pathways off the lobby are usually straightforward and the lobby space usually well defined, but in the case of Vegas these demarcations are deliberately confusing, blurring the edge between what is lobby and what is game-floor, even between what is outdoors and what is indoors. Although Philippe Starck has played with this idea of the lobby affording both indoor and outdoor space, nowhere does it push these boundaries more than in Vegas, where it literally spills out of the doors.

Check-in desk

The check-in desk has also evolved as the new contemporary hotels aim for seamless exchange of information between guest and hotel.

Apart from the mega hotels of Vegas that are designed to accommodate enough guests to fill their 3000 rooms (occupancy rates hover at an average of 90%) and resemble more an airport check-in area, most new designs have opted for a more 'homely' approach.

Desks might be a series of stand alone uncluttered tables set at low level, where guest and hotel employee sit at the same level (see Sheraton Miramar, Egypt) or may conform to a more traditional 'closed' unit where the division between guest and employee is more distinct.

Some resemble a 'bar' in the sense of a stand alone unit at elbow height and may act not only as platforms for pieces of wall-art (see Morrison,

Dublin; Four Seasons, Las Vegas) but may be considered works of art in their own right (see St Martins Lane, London).

Bedrooms

Hotel spaces may let you be who you want to be, without the usual constraints of domestic home life and routine. Moreover, hotel spaces, especially the bedroom, may allow you to dream about how your own home could be and show you how better to organise yourself and your things. Walk-in closets, for example, found in most of the Four Seasons hotels, are one of the design aspects that most of us dream of having in our own homes.

But we, as guests, also know that these rooms are not our own. They are not part of our daily lives, and so we feel free to behave as we wish (within reason), making as much mess as we like knowing that shortly after we leave the bed will look as though it had never been slept in.

The rooms are not ours, but at the same time we do not want them to have been anybody else's. The worst thing to happen when entering a hotel room for the first time is to find some article or strand of hair belonging to the previous guest. We do not want to find any ghosts in the closet, and so designers must create designs that complement the work of the chambermaid. The room must simulate the idea of 'no history'.

The room must also carry the theme of the hotel while retaining a very distinct feel of privacy. The first boutique hotel, Morgans of New York, was also perhaps the first to demonstrate this by echoing the chequerboard theme throughout the interior design and furnishing of the rooms, a theme that was stamped out explicitly in the lobby entrance.

In contrast, some of the more mega-resorts have maybe placed too much emphasis on 'theming' in public areas and have lost their way with the rooms, ending up with bland international designs that could be found anywhere in the world (see the mega-hotels of

Vegas). Other smaller scale projects manage to achieve this balance by designing in unique details for each room (Hotel Albergo, Beirut) and/or making the guest feel part of the design process (St Martins Lane, London).

Comfort, safety, quiet and privacy are key no matter how big or small the room volume is, whether city or resort. In addition, the rooms must be 'smart', incorporating creatively the use of technology – whether external gadgets or in-built systems.

Smart rooms

Designers of new hotels have had to educate themselves about the daily use of new and fast technologies, especially for those constantly on the move. Fax/modem ports are essential requirements for the bedroom and are ideally placed in a discreet but convenient way avoiding cable spaghetti, and with access to a decent sized working surface to rest the laptop/ phone/gadget.

However, this 'office within a room', unless in a suite (where a 'study' area is detached) must be subtle and discreet. Solutions have included a fold out table, or table with many pull-out surfaces (see One Aldwych, London) that can be put away after use, allowing the bedroom to be a relaxing haven once again. The designer must consider this use of bedroom as part-time 'personal office' from the outset.

The 'smart phone' is another piece of technology that comes in the new hotel package and as it now facilitates sophisticated operations, it must also be given a place in the room that is convenient to sit at or stand with.

Lighting switches and choices must also be 'smart' and obvious. Guests do not want to have their intelligence challenged by a complicated lighting system that turns one light off and the other on at the same time. 'Smart' lighting systems may have the potential to allow the guest to individualise his room, and designers have the opportunity to exploit these gadgets.

For example, one of the new contemporary hotels allows the guest to choose the colour of lighting above the bed (see St Martins Lane, London).

Bathrooms

Bathrooms are becoming the prize piece for some hotels, especially where space is at a premium. The 'temple of beauty' may offer deep tubs, his and hers washbasins, walk-in showers, Italian marble and hip chrome finishings. From the amusing details of Starck's pointy wash basins at the Paramount Hotel, New York, to Solfield's metro-tiled urban bathrooms at the SoHo Grand, New York, to the all singing and dancing 'sanctuaries of retreat' at the Four Seasons hotels internationally, bathrooms are high on the list of marketing attractions for the weary traveller.

Hyatt customer support research reported (1998) that guests spend 25% of the time in their room in the bathroom, hence the call for a well designed, functional and yet comfortable bathroom space that may also carry the hotel theme or narrative. Not such an easy task with limited space and limited budget.

Attention to minute and less costly details may make for a great bathroom when the budget is stretched. For example, at the Albergo Hotel, Beirut, elaborately decorated glass Damascene bowls are generously filled with bath salts from the Dead Sea, with a glass scoop to deliver them to the hot deep tub. An inexpensive and yet luxurious detail that can make a big difference from the usual Cellophane wrapped soap or thimble-full of artificially coloured perfumed salts.

High-tech can also meet bathroom, as showcased at the One Aldwych, London, where a mini-tv screen projects out of the side of the washbasin on one side with the shaving mirror projecting on the other.

Space is also another and very important design consideration and in the city hotels, bathrooms can be a squeeze. For example, in

Starck's bathroom designs at the Royalton, New York, there are no decent sized surfaces left available upon which to place the wash bag. At the Grand Hyatt Berlin an illusion of space is created through the use of two wide entrances to the bathroom – one that leads to the bedroom and the other to the corridor. The bathroom then becomes a room in its own right rather than an add on to the main bedroom.

Restaurant and bars

'Fine-dining' and 'hip-bars' have taken an increasingly more important role as hotels market their restaurants and bars as separate from the hotel. Great care and attention are paid to their creation and often they stand out as unique works of design. The restaurants Nobu at The Metropolitan Hotel, London, and the Picasso at Bellagio, Las Vegas are two of the more grand but contemporary examples; but throughout the projects presented here, and most are concentrated in the new contemporary city hotels, the restaurant and bar offer other focal points for design besides the lobby.

The restaurants and bars may have their own design identity and colour themes that are distinct from the hotel's overall theme (see Oriel at the Mandalay Bay, Las Vegas) or may incorporate explicitly elements of the hotel's design themes (see SoHo Grand, New York; Hotel Zebra, Paris).

Even entrances to the hotel's restaurants and bars do not necessitate a walk through the hotel itself, reflecting the growing trend for hotels to design for the local market, although there will be at least one access route to and from the lobby for the hotel guest.

Spaces in between

Corridors, elevators, doors and staircases, are other spaces to platform design and are increasingly being creatively used to carry design themes. Whether as a showcase for local art (see below), for creative lighting designs (see elevators at One Aldwych, London), affording another surface upon which to decorate (see elevators Four Seasons, New York), displaying unique door designs (see SoHo Grand, New York) or carrying its own story from floor to floor (see staircase in Albergo, Beirut), every space available can be used as an expression of design. And it is often here, in the less obvious spaces, where attention paid to detailed design can really create a stir.

Hotel as art gallery

Another trend emerging is the role of the hotel interior as a platform for art. At one extreme, a complete gallery has been designed within the hotel itself at the Bellagio Hotel, Las Vegas, hosting an impressive collection of early 19th century European art; at another is the incredible collection of Picasso originals in the Picasso restaurant (also at the Bellagio Hotel, Las Vegas). At a more modest scale, walls in many hotels are being used to display works by known local artists but keeping their place in the background (see SoHo Grand, New York; the Morrison, Dublin); others are actually allocating almost gallery-type spaces for art works (see the Salon Blanc, Hotel Square, Paris).

In keeping with this trend, in his hotel designs Philippe Starck is increasingly using the lobby as a stage for eclectic pieces of sculpture and furniture, both old and new, and is placing them in such a way that the space resembles a gallery for contemporary art installations.

Other rooms . . .

Business centres, spa and fitness centres, ballrooms and conference facilities, though increasingly important as add on functions to the new hotel, have not been included in detail in this book.

Individualisation

More and more hotels boast unique design in every room. While this may be true for some of the more intimate hotels whose philosophy and budget pivot around individualisation (see Hotel Albergo, Beirut, where every room is unique in every way). In the case of the larger hotels this often means simply the slight tweaking of one or two elements that will qualify each room as unique. Whether it is bed linen, colour themes, bathroom tiles or art on the walls, a unique difference – no matter how small – appeals to the guest's sensibilities: being seen as an individual, rather than just a room number.

At one extreme, Michael Graves, responsible for the architecture and interiors of the Sheraton Miramar Hotel in Egypt, hoped that the guest would identify the room with the colour and geometrical shape in which it was housed rather than simply by number. At a more discrete level, guests might be treated to one-off pieces of furniture or wall art or even art-headboards (Paramount Hotel, NYC) in keeping with the hotel's overall theme. In one of the most recently designed hotels (St Martins Lane, London) guests have even been empowered with the choice over lighting – which, in this particular case, contributes to the overall look of the hotel when viewed from the street outside.

Access: point and click
Travelling to the far reaches of the globe has become easier, faster and more affordable pushing passenger figures up and up and hotel occupancy rates higher and higher. Other worlds have come closer, distances have shortened, and brand names are now found everywhere.

Familiarity breeds comfort and the owners and designers of new hotels have wisened up to this fact, giving the guest brand name furniture designs, artworks, linens or toiletries, as comfort-blankets within a foreign environment. For example, Donna Karan home products found in the room are now also on sale in the hotel lobby; Aveda body care products available in the bathrooms are also on sale at the hotel's spa; postcards of Philippe Starck's hotel designs are for sale in the lobby of the same hotel.

Not only has travel itself eased but arranging the travel itinerary has also become easier. With access to the internet, and more publications on our shelves than ever before, we now have vast amounts of detailed information about places and spaces, no matter how remote, at our fingertips.

Hotels may now not just be booked through the internet, but may also be viewed on-line. There is also an increasing amount of image based publications springing up dedicated to hotel design – the editions produced by Design Destinations International; and such books as *Hip Hotels City* (Thames & Hudson), *Hip Hotels Escape* (Thames & Hudson), *Hotel Design* (Laurence King) etc.

Thus, the guest may see, in advance of arrival, what the rooms and public spaces look like, influencing his choice over one place over another. The way that the interiors come across on-line also becomes important for marketing the hotel.

Chapters
The first four chapters of this book look at a variety of contemporary hotel designs for the city and how each hotel's identity is expressed through new design ideas. The expression of this design narrative is seen in its most subtle and luxurious form in the work included in the first chapter, Contemporary City; it is at its most discreet in the work included in the chapter Intimate; it is most clearly expressed in the work of designer Philippe Starck in his designs for hotelier Ian Schrager in the chapter Hotel as Theatre; and is an idea diluted across a chain of hotels that has branded the idea of hip design, in the chapter Branding the Boutique.

Moving on from the city the following chapter on Hybrids presents three examples of where a non-interior designer has been asked to develop the interior designs of a hotel. The three projects are different in all respects but for this common idea and may represent the way forward for hoteliers looking for a non-typical and non-brand approach to hotel design. The work of fashion designers and film set designers is showcased here in distinctly different settings with very different outcomes.

In the chapter New for Old three projects are presented which have all adapted an old building into a new hotel. The original function of the building – in these cases a prison, a convent and a car factory – can often dominate the overall interior architecture of the building, giving the interiors a ready-made identity. These three projects demonstrate how designers have worked with the original character and designs of the building, and woven in their own creative design solutions.

We then move into the Other World of Las Vegas where the work of the designer is on a scale like no other. Four hotels are presented of which three base their design philosophy on 'replicature' – the idea of replicating places, cities, worlds – and the fourth acts as a 'haven' for design within the bizarre context of resort-city. The introduction to this chapter details the bizarre and fantastical context in which such design is taking place.

Following from this is one very strong example of a Contemporary Resort where a named architect and designer – Michael Graves – was asked to put his design stamp in a more remote part of our typical world.

The chapter Atrium presents four stunning examples of the use of the atrium structure in hotels. Working from the outside in rather than from the inside out as we have in all the other chapters, these projects demonstrate how the interior designer has had to 'humanise' the scale and designs of otherwise vast and cold spaces.

Our last chapter presents two New Classic hotels located in two of the world's most international cities, New York and London. The approach is so explicitly a mix of the contemporary with the classical in every respect – from materials, to lines, to furnishings and motifs – that the New Classic label, implying as it does a long shelf-life is justified.

All projects are introduced by a few core facts – the date completed, number of rooms, number of floors, and building type, if appropriate, to aid quick search by those categories. Then follows the 'hotel soundbite' – a one-liner pulled directly from the hotel's press release or brochure – that sums up the way in which the hotel itself would like to be seen (not applicable for the chapter Atrium). This may help or hinder opinion, or may even be amusing.

But before the projects, a few words from hoteliers and designers behind the scenes in Talks.

talks

HOTELS FOR THE 21ST CENTURY

**Interview with American hotel owner and entrepeneur,
Ian Schrager of Morgans, Royalton, Paramount, Delano,
Mondrian, St Martins Lane**

Ian Schrager pioneered the first of the known 'boutique' hotels in New York in the early 1980s by paying deliberate attention to design details and themes, and challenging the usual functions of typical hotel spaces. After working on Morgans Hotel with French designer Andrée Putman, he teamed up with internationally renowned designer Philippe Starck with the aim of re-inventing the concept of hotel and its role in the local, as well as the international, design conscious communities.

Beginnings

'When I started in the hotel business in 1982 the landscape was completely different. It was a time when hotels had been taken over by real estate developers and pitched at the mass-market, with a rubber-stamp model of design that was easy to execute. This mass-marketing and chaining took the spirit out of interior spaces and their designs.

'I wanted to give hotels something new. Something that was personal with a sense of humour, wit, reverence, spirit and each hotel with a unique identity. I wanted to move away from being just a place for sleep to a place that

*Lobby of Morgans Hotel, New York,
the first of Ian Schrager's hotels.*

could be uplifting, rich and rewarding. The challenge was to attach visuals to these ideas.

'I have been working with Philippe Starck since 1985 and it is a relationship that is continually evolving. As a team we aim to do something that is different and exciting. Something on the cutting edge that will stand the test of time and not fade with bad taste alongside the popular fashion trends.

'When we looked back historically to the first ideas of hotels, bars, inns, we found that typically in the big cities, the hotel hosted some of the major events of that city (marriages, functions, celebrations) and had an important role in the local community.'

New use of old space

'Our first hotel (Morgans NYC) did not have a lobby. It emphasised quiet, calm, discretion. It was purposely understated, anonymous, but sophisticated in design. With our subsequent projects we started to look at the use of the public spaces as a way of adding an extra dimension to the hotel. Each new project is like starting again from square one, and we try to individualise the themes and designs more and more.

'When you visit a new city and you stay in a place that you don't live in, you want to visit the places where the local city people go. This is what we have tried to create in our hotels. The lobby, for example, is a bee hive of activity and acts as a microcosm of the city you are in, recreating the sense of the "local" within a space occupied by non-locals. A place where fun is high on the agenda and the fact that there are a hundred or so rooms on top of you, is incidental rather than the focus. It is a place for socialising, for eating and drinking, with great food and exciting visuals.'

Hotels for the 21st century

'Today, the introduction of the internet has shifted the power in the market from the seller to the buyer. The buyer now has more choice than before and we are trying to complement this new aspect of modern life in our hotel designs by providing the guest with more choice over his environment. For example, being able to change the colour of the lights in the rooms according to individual taste (St Martins Lane). We are working on the concept of flexibility in design and at the same time trying to humanise it.

'Our next project in London – the Sanderson- will be our first Urban Spa, that aims to combine great cities with the "cure". Why not be able to visit a great city like London and go home feeling better than when you arrived? We have high culture in the city but away from the mountains, the sea and good air. The Urban Spa will bring both worlds into one, emphasising well-being in the heart of the city.

CITY LUXURIES

**Interview with hotel owner and designer Gordon Campbell Grey
of One Aldwych, London**

Gordon Campbell Grey travelled the world while working in the hotel business in search of the exact design criteria that could make the perfect hotel. He bases his ideas around the theme of luxury.

Luxury

'What is luxury? Is it something you can buy, like a Gucci handbag, or is it an ambience of absolute calm and tranquillity? I feel that luxury is better defined as a tactile experience that encompasses a great sense of comfort, and we then bathe that comfort in wonderful design.

'At One Aldwych we designed the spaces, the furnishings, the objects, the lighting, to allow the guest to feel this comfort and luxury but not to feel intimidated or overwhelmed by it.

'After travelling around the hotels of the world I was looking for a template for a good hotel. Throughout my search I found that originality and individuality were missing. Everything looked the same, all the details were the same.

'Hotels, as an industry, had been slow to change in image and outlook. Most hoteliers, for

Lobby of One Aldwych, London.

example, were uninteresting and uninterested people, and winded up as operators of the hotel, which is not such a creatively stimulating job. The only example we had of a 'designed' hotel was the country house hotel. But to transfer these designs, that were perhaps the only hotels that were distinctive in style and design, on a larger scale and in the city is a difficult project.'

A new breed of unique hotel design

'I have an allergy to the dripping deluxe of 5 star hotels. It expresses an attitude of snobbery so much so that you feel you have to be properly dressed and with the right Louis Vuitton luggage to go there!

'There has been a shift. Hotel management, that used to be very unfashionable, even boring, has changed. Now big personalities are on the scene attracting celebrity names, which then subsequently come to be associated with the hotel. A new breed of hotels has sprung up and [they] are all trying to make their mark. I am not referring to the boutique hotels, but more to the state of the art all-singin'-all-dancin' hotel that is also a snob-free zone!

'People these days are seeking out individuality in design more and more. In five or six years time a few companies around the world will own everything and this will encourage people to seek out design and places that are not branded with an international signature.'

A home away from home?

'The philosophy of One Aldwych is one of exquisite quality down to every last detail. Simple but perfect, discreet but fresh. Our primary aim is comfort and luxury, and we have achieved this through lacing our contemporary designs with Classicism.

'One Aldwych is not trying to be a "home away from home". We want to offer something different from home. We offer an uncluttered space that is calm and a service that allows anonymity for our guests. We try to be perfect all the way through for all 140 guests, which is not such an easy task.

'The lobby is the centre point of the hotel, and I like to keep some sense of theatre to the space as you have in the more traditional grand hotels like the Savoys of this world. We provide a different space from those but we still retain some dramatic aspects to the space and the sculptures that occupy it.'

Time and place

'We are not stuck in the world of dry-sherry-sipping in the lobby bar, but we feel we have brought some aspects of London culture into this space. The grand windows of the lobby look out to the busy junction of Aldwych and are always painted with London's traffic of red buses and black cabs that give the guest the sense of location.

'These designs are not just for this moment, but will stand the test of time. We want to be considered a "modern classic" and not just a fashionable trendy thing of the late 90s.

'The pool in the basement is one of the most loved things by our guests for its colours and lights; but also our technological facilities in each room are often postively commented upon. As technology advances and computers reduce in size, human interaction through service will become even more important.

'This is a very interesting phase for hotel designers. The customers' needs are changing pace as technology affords different capabilities, and developments in interior designs must keep up with this.'

DESIGNING CLASSICISM IN VEGAS

Interview with Charles Gruwell, design director of Avery Brooks & Associates about the classical designs for the Four Seasons, Las Vegas, in the context of the casino city

The design

'We have coined the term "transitional design". We define it by the non-use of ultra modern materials like chrome, glass, metals, and the non-use of traditional themes like English and Italian styles. We rest it on clean classical designs that draw from the genre of Classicism but are interpreted to fit the modern day lifestyle. Our designs have classical bones but with a fresh new look.

'For example, we might use fringing and tassels on drapes but the materials will be contemporary. The woodwork is traditional but the carpets upon which the work lays are contemporary. We use contemporary and appetising colours – deep aubergines with saffron and cinnamon. The light fixtures are mainly glass but we may use a traditional shade. We put couches in the suites so people can lie and read a book, and we might use a fabric that you might find in someone's home.

'We want to bring peace, tranquillity and comfort to our designs throughout all spaces – rooms, corridors and the lobby.'

Lobby of Four Seasons, Las Vegas.

The guest

'The Four Seasons guest is very distinctive. Usually very private, well travelled and discerning. They come here because they want the fun of Las Vegas but the tranquillity of a luxurious residence. That is what we aim to provide in our designs, so that people feel like they are coming home.

'Our guests travel a lot and are knowledgeable about cultures and history, past and present. We have incorporated luxury that has its roots in the past, but in a style that is transitional rather than stuck in history. And this is a style that can work all over the world.'

Hotel as home

'One of the most important elements to "hotel as home" is scale. You have to be very careful in your designs not to be too grandiose or mega. The size of things can determine whether the room feels personal or not. We try to be the counterpoint to mega with residentially scaled furniture and spaces. We have put things in the rooms here that you might find typically in someone's bedroom as part of a "personal" collection of things.

'The hotel does not have to be like *my* home but rather like *a* home. Themed hotels have a specific aim to capture a certain theme throughout. Business hotels are predominantly used for business functions and by business people; they might be attractive but are primarily function-oriented.

'The Four Seasons brief is to bring home-like qualities into the hotel. For example, the furniture in the rooms is not picked to match but rather picked like an eclectic mix of furniture collected over the years that you would find typically in a home.

'Comfort and luxury are key to our designs. We do not want our guests to feel that they are in a hotel as hotels in the past have been known to be cold in style and unwelcoming. We want our guests to feel as relaxed as though they are in their own homes.'

Local context

'Here in Vegas we had a theme to influence us from the next door Mandalay Bay Hotel and Casino which we also designed. We let some of the ancient Asian themes of that hotel drift through to the Four Seasons in the form of Asian artefacts in the rooms and the corridors. Inspiration for design also comes from the location we are in, which we then combine with classical lines.

'Vegas is known for its fantasy, for suspending time in reality, for transfixing the guest all over the world. It's Vegas, but it also wants to be the world. Las Vegas is not about intimacy and discretion. It is bold and playful.

'The Four Seasons, however, has its own design agenda, and simply put is "modern but traditional". It has a very distinctive class of design that is recognised globally and we must respect this within the Vegas context.

'Other hotels in Vegas are phenomenal in size and concept. We aim instead to be intimate, quiet, discreet. A home away from home in Vegas.'

The world of Vegas

'Vegas? It is like a design laboratory and is becoming better known from West to East Coast for its fine designers and restaurateurs. These top restaurant designers – like Adam Tihany and Tony Chee – have brought with them international interior design. It keeps on reinventing itself, always shifting emphasis and diversifying themes.

'Can you have good designs and slot machines sitting side by side? Yes, you can marry the two. The new Vegas visitor is more upmarket than before and desires good design as well as the opportunity to have fun on the games floor. Here we have the best of both worlds as we share the access to the casino with the Mandalay Bay Hotel next door.

'Las Vegas is the ultimate playground for adults. An entertainment Mecca. Shows, theatre, gambling, girls. It is the City of the Millennium but still based ultimately on gambling with sun all year round. It is a city that excites the child within you.'

WORKING WITH THE VERNACULAR

Interview with American architect and designer Michael Graves on the interior designs of the Sheraton Miramar Hotel, Egypt

Internationally renowned architect and designer Michael Graves was asked by the client to take as source the vernacular designs of rural Egypt and create a design vocabulary out of these elements combined with Graves' own post-modern ideas.

Looking around the local village centre that was designed to typify Egyptian rural vernacular architecture (by graduates of Hassan Fathy), Graves used these dome and vault forms as the point of departure for design. The most clear example of this homage to the vernacular are perhaps the guest room domes which have remained in raw brick, the bed positioned directly underneath affording a 'raw' awakening for guests.

The brief
'I had a conversation with the client about his expectations and the reality of what the local crafts people could be expected to produce. The client was not specific about the nature of the pieces except to say that we should not pretend that the craft community could produce fine furniture. The character of the pieces for each of the guest rooms as well as public spaces came originally from us, with critical evaluation by the client.'

Lobby of Sheraton Miramar Hotel.

Ideals and realities

'I thought that we should be sympathetic to the possibilities offered by the furniture makers – meaning they should not be overly taxed in terms of precision. Therefore we attempted to make furniture which might be called, to some extent, *rustici* (in the sense of basic and hand-made.)

'I have always been interested in early Egyptian furniture, as it leads to both Greek and Roman furniture. That interest develops mostly from the anamorphic character of many of the basic elements such as chairs and tables.

'I am also fascinated with their early Egyptian accommodation to the construction of the architecture relative to how furniture might adapt to it. By this I mean that a long rectangular table might have only three legs – two at one end and one at the other – because floors were often rough and uneven and three points determined the plane; so much better than our standard four legs of today.'

Egyptian inspirations

'While the furniture that we have designed is not explicitly Egyptian, I do feel that its rustic character gives it both an archaic and vernacular quality. While the exterior of the buildings have much of my personality in them, we have tried nevertheless to use a similar strategy as we did in the furniture, and that is to be sympathetic to the constructional possibilities and vernacular methods, which has led us and the project to, I think, interesting tangencies to the local character and context.

'In terms of stuccoing versus leaving bare certain brick elements, we attempted to persuade the client to leave many of the domes and vaults bare brick, as we feel that the construction of these architectural elements is so wonderfully made that it would lessen the whole if some of these roofs were not left exposed.'

Colours, textures and stripes

'We chose colours that from the day they were painted to the present time, would fade from the original rather bright colours, to faded colours that exposure to the intense sun brings about. We think that the stucco surfaces when rendered in this manner take on a patina that links them more closely with their climate.

'The stripes used on the stucco vault in the dining room are a rather explicit reference to tents, as I have always loved the kind of light that comes through the canvas of tents, especially while dining.'

Textiles

'Textile designs were tailored to local manufacturing availability and capability but we also started the process of fabric selection by going through our own fabric library and finding designs that either we had made previously or others already produced that were in keeping with the archaic character of the project.

'It is by virtue of colour, fabrics, textures etc. that broad surfaces – in a bedspread or drapery, for example – have the ability to convey character as much as any group of furnishings. Therefore we thought that these qualities were crucial in terms of conveying themes already discussed.'

Lighting

'I thought it was important to be explicit about the lights that were seen as our design, and therefore modern, versus those that were traditionally based.

'I was fascinated by other projects that the client had built using traditional lighting and felt that their character was absolutely appropriate for some of the public spaces, especially the restaurants. Therefore for these spaces, we let the local lighting designer make proposals to us for our review. In the guest rooms, we designed special lights to illuminate the vaults and domes that were, again, minimal in character, as well as reading lights which, in hotel design, become a kind of condition required by the guest.'

contemporary city

Contemporary designs for urban living; calm and neutral palettes but mixed with bright and playful detail of colour; quality linens and luscious textiles; creative lighting and eclectic furniture; works of fine art and contemporary sculpture; intriguing corridors and intimate details . . . and all set in the heart of the city.

All of this and more combined modestly and typically in the adaptation of an existing building or structure, with moderate room numbers and limited public space volumes. These hotels specialise in giving fine attention to creative details while answering the needs of the technology equipped guest. They take pride in themselves for the resulting mix that fits in the local context (attracting local clientele) and satisfies the international traveller too.

Often described as 'temples of contemporary style in the heart of the city', they also instantiate a slice of that city culture typically in the lobby, restaurants and bars of the hotel.

This chapter presents four recent projects from London, New York and Berlin, each set in the heart of their own city and clearly stamping aspects of their city on their design approach.

ONE ALDWYCH, London

Interior design: GORDON CAMPBELL GRAY AND MARY FOX-LINTON OF FOX-LINTON ASSOCIATES
1998   105 rooms

'a contemporary luxury hotel in the centre of London'

The One Aldwych is a one-off original hotel, comfortable and luxurious with many intriguing creative details throughout public and private spaces.

Designed by hotelier Gordon Campbell Gray and designer Mary Fox-Linton of Fox-Linton Associates, the hotel does not overstate its contemporary design features but rather weaves them in and out of a discreet but fresh ambience of detail and comfort. Housed in a 1907 Edwardian building on a triangular site at the junction of the Strand and Aldwych, the building was originally home to the *Morning Post* newspaper.

Modernised in 1977, it opened as the One Aldwych hotel in 1998 and now houses 93 guest rooms and 12 suites, two restaurants, two bars and a coffee bar, a health and fitness centre with pool, meeting rooms and a 30 seater private screening room for media professionals. Each space is distinctive in its own right and the restaurants, bars and gym clubs attract local clientele as well as hotel guests.

The light and expansive lobby is decorated with sculptures and tall glass plinths supporting

Entrance to One Aldwych.

exquisite floral displays. Chairs are high backed and coloured green taupes, oranges, mauves; and Andre Wallace's distinctive sculpture of a bronze man in dinghy with long padels sits to one side. Steel mesh panels frame the back wall facing into the triangular point of the bar, which is finished in black lacquer and the chairs in black leather in contrast to the bright, light spaces of the lobby and its tall glass tubes.

Everywhere there is meticulous attention to detail; down to the interiors of the elevators which are carefully designed with chequered mirrors and illuminated in lime green by day or soft lilac by night.

One restaurant space – the Axis – is dominated by a walled mural by English artist Robert Walker. In contrast the Indigo restaurant, located on the mezzanine level overlooking the lobby, is furnished with chenille covered chairs hugging a steel mesh wall. The much talked about 18 metre long pool is decorated with bright blue mosaic tiles, stainless steel water walls and swimming comes with underwater music!

Rooms are dominated by clean lines, luxurious linens and simple colours. All High-tech facilities are integrated discreetly including a fibre optic reading light and a small TV screen next to the washbasin in the bathroom.

Details of the lobby. Light and airy with sculptures, glass plinths and the high-backed chairs looking out of the grand windows on to London's traffic.

Details of the Axis Restaurant mural on the back wall and curvey staircase.

Cool coffee at the Cinnamon Bar with high black stools and metallic finishings.

Details of the guest bedrooms.
Simple linens, natural
calm colours, and High-tech.
TV screen by the washbasin
in the bathroom.

Detail of guest corridor. Soft discreet lighting throughout.

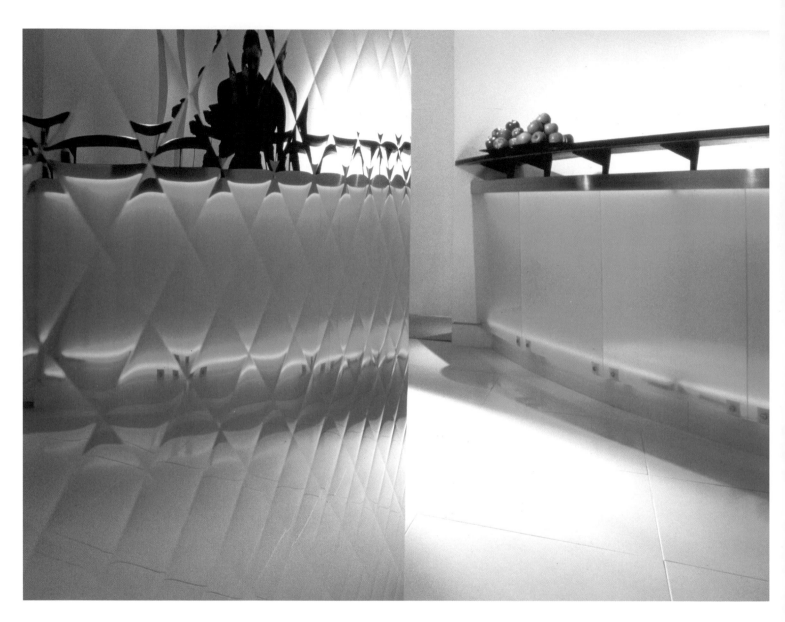

Door detail of health club on lower ground floor, reflecting the reception desk's light on the 'quilted' panels of the door.

Details of the 18-metre swimming pool decorated with blue mosaics and a yellow back wall, screened off by glass walls and doors.

SOHO GRAND, New York

Interior design: WILLIAM SOLFIELD OF SOLFIELD STUDIOS

1996   369 rooms   16 floors

'chic without attitude'

A new structure with 16 storeys rises tall in this otherwise low-rise district of trendy downtown New York and was the first hotel to be built in SoHo for more than a century.

Solfield, himself a SoHo based designer, looked to local history for inspiration, taking the best of SoHo's architecture, art and lifestyle from the late 19th century through to the 20th, recreating an Art Deco ambience of a 1930s New York hotel but with the occasional industrial-led surprise.

Comfort is secured through a series of well thought through design themes that make subtle reference to the city, but that also breaks the mould of more typical historical stereotypes. The cast-iron grand staircase which leads to the first floor reception, for example, is actually suspended (reference to the city's bridges) and is dotted with back-lit Coca-Cola glass bottle rounds (traditionally used on the inner edge of New York's sidewalks); the focal point of the Grand Canal restaurant is a large mercury-mirror butler's ball that hangs in the centre, continuing the interplay of light carried throughout the hotel by antique and quicksilver mirrors. Local artists' work can also be found throughout the public spaces and rooms; some guest doors have been individualised by local artist Nancy Lorenz with patterns of hand painted silver-leaf.'

The red brick entrance and two level lobby is anchored by massive red brick columns and linked by an impressive cast-iron staircase that is suspended by two enormous cables at the back. Bottle glass discs are used to light each individual stair. It is worth noticing that the lobby is located on the first floor due to local flood-risk regulations.

The first floor lobby is divided between the check-in desk, which is home to an enormous public clock, and the lounge. Naturally lit with its 16ft floor to ceiling windows and softened by chocolate coloured velvet drapes, the space is host to an assortment of large and comfortable furniture, tropical palms, William Morris textiles and some oversized draughtsman lamps. The entire area is decorated with mercury mirrors embedded with chicken wire and cast stone columns supporting a ceiling of riveted beams.

The Grand Bar of mirror panels and comfortable leather padded bar stools also hosts an incredible light from the 1940s/50s that was salvaged from a surgeon's operating theatre, of twelve bare bulbs under an umbrella of panelled dark mirrored glass.

Elevator cabs are decorated with wire glass panels and a mica ceiling.

The Chartroom and private dining area takes its name from the collection of antique maps and nautical charts displayed there. Custom fabrics share a neutral palette with champagne velvet drapes, hand rubbed wood work and burnished walls. The underlying theme of exploration and discovery is accentuated by its extraordinary handmade carpet, featuring Eastern and Western Hemispheres floating in a starry blue cosmos.

The 16th floor penthouses offer dramatic views, to the south taking in Lower Manhattan and the World Trade Center and to the north the Empire State and Chrysler Buildings. Rooms demonstrate understated luxury using a neutral palette of taupes, mushroom, greens and beige. Furniture is custom made, finishings in raw woods or glass. Drapes and bed throws are of deep coloured velvet. Bringing the urban context into the the bathrooms are white oblong tiles, top to bottom, of the type found in the New York City subway.

THE METROPOLITAN, London

Interior design: KEITH HOBBS AND LINZI COPPICK OF UNITED DESIGNERS
1997   155 rooms

'meeting the needs of the modern traveller'

Answering the needs of the modern traveller for a contemporary, central and affordable hotel in the middle of London, United Designers have used a mixture of contemporary designs with classical materials. Simple but elegant lines have been created using marbles, hardwoods and a muted palette of plain and natural fabrics, with little ornamentation. The overall design result is cool, calm and luxurious.

Both the Metropolitan and the Halkin Hotels, London, are owned by Christina Ong and have similar design themes – cool, calm, sleek and sophisticated. The Halkin (featured in the chapter Intimate) has the more discreet reputation featuring the highly regarded Stefano Cavallini restaurant, while the Metropolitan is better known for its trendy and popular Met Bar and Nobu restaurant, both slap bang in the centre of busy London.

The Metropolitan, the first new hotel on Park Lane, London, for 20 years, also houses the Michelin starred 'new style' Japanese Nobu restaurant, and is becoming known as the 'coolest' hotel in town. The Donna Karan designed uniforms for Metropolitan staff perhaps say it all.

Plain walls, plain fabrics and soft curves bring an immediate feeling of calm into the lobby/lounge area. A sculptural wall clock in light grey tones is the only piece of ornamentation to the walls, and on the floors a selection of Helen Yardley commissioned rugs in subdued tones.

The lobby shop stocks pieces of
Donna Karan homeware and other
hotel accessories.

The Met Bar, that attracts local Londoners as well as visiting guests, features acid-etched glass, curved polished walls and an upbeat abstract New York skyline mural inspired by Jean Michel Basquiat. Chocolate browns and deep reds contrast with the modern tubular steel bar front and curved red 'lava' top.

Rooms host a mixture of plain fabrics, plain blinds and blind walls using soft mauve and olive upholstery combined with pear wood furnishings and fittings. The latest electronic facilities are subtly hidden in the wood headboards.

Some bathrooms feature a free standing bath with pear wood surround.

The Nobu restaurant is sparsely decorated, light and airy. Olive tones complement the pear wood furnishings and the black dining chairs were inspired by Frank Lloyd Wright's designs.

GRAND HYATT BERLIN, Berlin

Interior architecture: JOSÉ RAFAEL MONEO

Interior design: HANNES WETTSTEIN OF 9D DESIGN OF ZURICH

1998   340 rooms

**'contemporary and timeless elegance . . .
with the latest in technology'**

The Grand Hyatt Berlin, superbly located at the Potsdamer Platz in the heart of busy Berlin, is a hotel of clarity and function but with contemporary tastes and comfort. It could easily lead the new breed of business hotels in its successful combination of strong design with its excellent information facilities – the 24 hour business centre, fax/modem ports, three ISDN lines and internet access in every room.

The interior space pivots around an enclosed atrium that allows an interesting play of light and shadow in among a pair of inverted crystal-shaped pyramids that jut into this space at right angles from the ceiling. The 'grand' marble staircase rises from the foyer to the banqueting floor where from the balcony guests can view Berlin's Marlene Dietrich Platz and Alts Potsdamer Strasse.

The lobby lounge incorporates the restaurant 'Tizian' with elegant wooden furniture, while the Vox restaurant, which has its own access as well as that from the hotel, is more like a large theatre kitchen featuring wood-burning ovens and open grills. Walls are polished red stucco with dark oak furniture and dark parquet floors creating a warm ambience.

The Bistro uses lighter cedar and beechwood with stainless steel, featuring dramatic red velvet drapes on the windows.

Guest rooms use cherrywoods – natural and dark stained – and the generous bathrooms with their large doors are pervaded by grey-blue granite and black marble for the wash stands. Clean and classic lines dominate and the overall feel is one of comfort without the fuss, while not being in any way minimal. Furniture is deliberately low to the floor, to afford a more spacious volume.

Art decorates the walls and each room has seven different black and white photographs taken from the Berlin Bauhaus archives.

The interior space pivots around an enclosed atrium that allows an interesting play of light and shadow in among a pair of inverted crystal-shaped pyramids that jut into this space at right angles from the ceiling.

The clean spacious lines of the lobby with
low level furniture.

Contemporary lines and furnishings of the lobby lounge and staircase.

Warm reds and dark woods in the Vox restaurant.

The long and elegant lines of the pool, overlooking Berlin.

*A warm but natural palette dominates the
guestrooms in contrast to the cool greys
and blues of the generous bathrooms.*

intimate

The five projects in this chapter describe hotels in the city that provide a more discreet and calm environment than those in the previous chapter. While lavishing attention on fine and contemporary design details, the ambience is clearly one of privacy and tranquillity. And each project offers intimacy and calm in its own way.

Historically, Hotel Montalembert in Paris was one of the first to cater for this new type of client, and its designs have often been used as reference for the new contemporary European city hotel. Designer Liaigre who worked on Montalembert later contributed to the Mercer, New York. Its contemporary lines and furnishings which are layered on to its original 1920s building are still strong and relevant today. The second project, the Albergo in Beirut offers an oriental-based contemporary intimacy combined with unique design, and is a hotel like no other in the way it roots its design references in its regional past. The Mercer of New York, and the Halkin of London offer some of the most understated luxury to be found in the heart of each city, with exquisite and calming design. Lastly and in contrast, The Hotel Square of Paris offers a richer palette of colours giving a more cosy ambience to its intimate corners.

HOTEL MONTALEMBERT, Paris

Interior design:
GRACE LEO ANDRIEU

FURNITURE BY: CHRISTIAN LIAIGRE
Completion 1990   56 rooms

'The stylish "must" of Paris' Left Bank where modernity and classicism combine'

Located in the heart of Paris the Hotel Montalembert, housed in its original hotel building of 1926, re-opened its doors in 1990 after a year long $8 million refurbishment. Owner and design director Andrieu aimed to create a hotel that combined a contemporary style with elements of luxury and elegant simplicity, and to weave this modern layer into the original fabric of the Hotel Montalembert that had existed for 70 years. She commissioned Liaigre to design one-off works of furniture and to restore original period pieces.

This play on the old with modern day themes, simple colours and rich textures has created a slick contemporary hotel with a sense of history and place.

The ground floor space – café, restaurant, library and bar – was carved out of a limited area but gives a series of fully functional independent spaces subtly differentiated by lighting levels.

Rooms tend to follow more classical Louis-Phillippe lines with modern luxurious fabrics and embroidered linens. The bathrooms boast deep bathtubs, marble floors, tall pivoting mirrors and state-of-the-art chrome fixtures.

Hallways and corridors are dominated by taupe and marine with light fixture design by sculptor Eric Schmitt.

From the lobby through to the staircase, the gentle colour scheme is carried through walls, carpeting and materials. Details of mirror and stand-alone pieces of furniture range from the Louis-Philippe style to the contemporary.

Detail of restaurant with sleek wooden tables and chairs, and striped covers.

Room details that combine an old comfortable atmosphere with the new contemporary style.

HOTEL ALBERGO, Beirut

Architect: JEAN-PIERRE MAGHARBANEÉ

*Interior design: TARFA SALAM, JACQUES GARCIA, JOUMMANA YOUSSEVITCH AND
NICOLE ASSEILY   1998   33 rooms   9 floors*

**'a modern and exotic hotel loaded with Oriental
references'**

Decorative, spangley, luxurious and historic. Part Oriental, part European and part Colonial. All these elements and more have been carefully crafted to create a hotel that is comfortably intimate and yet with a grand residential feel.

Hotel Albergo is located in the old and artistic quarter of Achrafiyeh in central Beirut, one of the quarters whose urban fabric has remained relatively undisturbed despite the brutal years of recent civil war. The building was originally a large villa built in the 1920s occupying four floors. Five floors were added in 1995 to make a nine-storey hotel with terrace and pool occupying the roof space, and a reputable Italian restaurant housed in the ground floor villa.

Four different designers worked on the interiors. Jacques Garcia was responsible for the entrance halls and lobby bar which occupy the ground floor, introducing Egyptian-Pharonic elements in terms of grand columns, temple lighting and stone statues, dressing the lobby bar and library in red velvets. The 33 suite-rooms, restaurant and other public spaces were individually designed by the London based Lebanese interior designer Tarfa Salam, who also

collaborated with Joummana Youssevitch on the bathrooms and with Nicole Asseily in the creation of the terrace.

Each room was carefully crafted using local elements in lighting and furnishings, each carrying its own theme. Expansive but intimate, each room too offers a space larger than a normal room, with individually chosen furnishings. Lavish detail has been paid to all elements, from the lights, colour themes, shades, cushions and carpets, all the way down to the door knobs on the closets.

The original room layout of the first four floors was retained and dominated the design of the subsequent five floors. The original floor tiles from the 1920s can still be seen on these initial floors and the designs led the theme for the rest of the hotel's floor designs.

Salam has drawn from all corners of the globe to create this luxurious and stimulating environment while keeping the designs firmly rooted in the local context. Furniture ranges from 19th century French and English to Ottoman and Damascene, combined with an incredible assortment of artefacts collected from the markets of Paris, London, Damascus, Istanbul and India. Some suites are dominated more by one theme than another (Turkish, French, Mediterranean or Damascene) with specifically themed details in terms of carpets, furniture or lighting.

The restaurant on the top floor is more like a living room than formal dining area. With an assortment of tables – from the calligraphic inscribed metal dishes of the Orient to the French dark wooded country dining tables, and a variety of cushioned high-back chairs and divans with an inviting mixture of coloured cushions, the overall theme remains strongly Oriental. Offering an eclectic mix of artefacts housed in glass cabinets, a stunning array of Syrian light fixtures and walls that display tiles with traditional Arabic calligraphy, the room could pass as a carefully curated design museum of the Orient.

All rooms are suites with warm comfortable living areas, spacious sleeping areas, and feature artefacts from throughout the Orient. Even the bed frames are individually sourced – this one above is detailed with Arabic calligraphy.

As with all bedrooms, all bathrooms are individually decorated and themed, combining marbles with wooden closets and an assortment of local artefacts.

Closets and cabinets are designed and styled based on original lattice woodwork.

Room numbers are individually painted and corridors decorated with images of the Orient – from Sultans to Princesses.

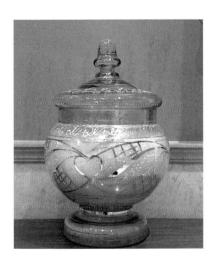

Glass pot of Dead Sea salts painted with gold Arabic calligraphy are placed in the bathroom.

Detail of Damascene chair featuring Mashrabeya woodwork.

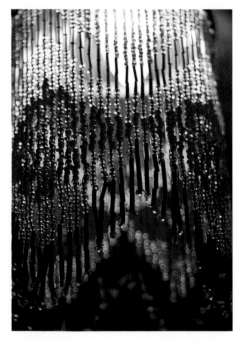

Huge and colourful Syrian-style chandeliers with clear and coloured glass beading dominate the bedrooms, with each room boasting a different light.

Walls are coloured plaster of terracotta reds and burnt oranges, lit colourfully with glass lamps while the more traditional glass beaded lamps cast elegant shadows on the wall.

The staircase is decorated with a fabulous assortment of characters from princes and princesses, sultans and amirs, dressed from the traditional to the flamboyant. Suggestions of Art Deco are found in the elegant curves of the blue painted iron balustrade and the stained glass windows on each floor.

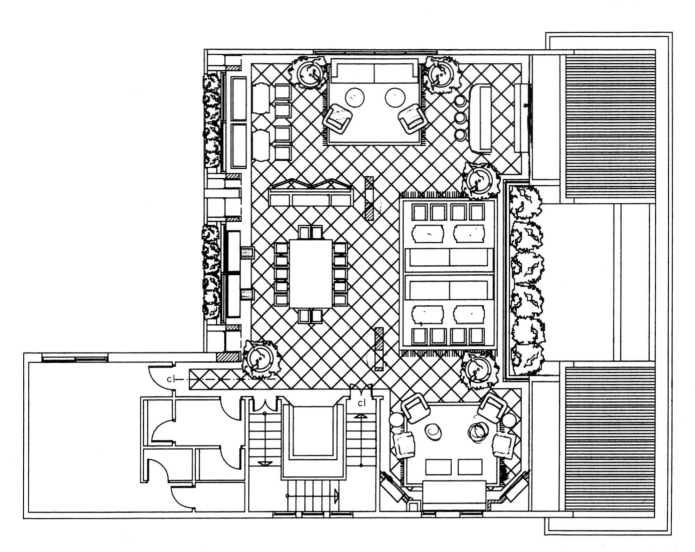

The restaurant is more like a living room with an incredible assortment of artefacts – old and new – including original calligraphic wall tiles.

The yellow, red, turquoise colour themes throughout the corridors and staircase continue up to the roof terrace and swimming pool.

Floor tiles from the original building were kept and can still be seen on the first four floors of the hotel.

THE MERCER HOTEL, New York

Interior design: CHRISTIAN LIAIGRE   1998   75 rooms   9 floors

'Zen and the art of hotel serenity'

Comfort and luxury in the heart of New York's SoHo district, the Mercer blurs the line between home and hotel. Owner Andre Balazs states: 'I wanted to conceive a hotel with an atmosphere of domestic bliss, a place you can walk into and not even realise you are in a hotel . . . but that also retains the character and history of SoHo.'

Intimate, with only 75 rooms on nine floors, the one hundred year old building went through a complete renovation by French interior designer Christian Liaigre (of Hotel Montalembert, Paris). The entire brickwork was refaced, cast iron columns restored, vaulting and gargoyles recovered, and original window mouldings rebuilt. Preserving ceiling heights, the Mercer is the first hotel to offer 'loft-living', with an abundance of natural light in the guest rooms affording a unique feeling of space, unusual in rooms in the heart of the city.

Overlooking the corner of Prince and Mercer, the 100 seat lobby entrance is distinctly intimate in scale with a domestic residential feel enhanced by its vintage book library, living room and bar. Furniture is crafted from dark African woods like wenge and ipe, sofas covered with elegant natural linens, simple lamps, affording in its entirety subtle and clean lines. Better known for his designs for the Hotel Montalembert on Paris's Left Bank, Christian Liaigre aims to 'soothe' with his interiors in his Zen quality styling.

Guest rooms open with long entrance hallways into loft-like spaces; high-ceiling bathrooms feature king-sized tubs and are clad in marble and white tiles.

Guest rooms open with long entrance hallways into loft-like spaces, high-ceiling bathrooms feature king-sized tubs and are clad in marble and white tiles.

THE HALKIN, London

Interior design: LABORATORIO ASSOCIATI   1998   41 rooms

'a secret haven in the heart of Belgravia'

With the dominating cream base, the mauves, redwoods and royal blues combine perfectly in the Halkin's cocktail bar

Combining the best of Italian minimal design, cool contemporary and state-of-the-art business facilities, the Halkin hotel sits very discreetly in a quiet side street in Belgravia, one of London's most upmarket areas. Sharp style, marbles and granite, sparse and spatial, Belgravia meets Italy.

Rooms are dominated by black, white and creams combined with the rosewood panelling, while bathrooms are 'palaces of shiny chrome'. The lobby's clean-cut pink and white marble floor is decorated with deep blue bucket armchairs. The staff fit the surrounds perfectly in their white Armani uniforms.

The discreet no-fuss exterior in a side street of Belgravia.

The renowned Stefano Cavallini restaurant in creams, soft mint green and rosewood furniture.

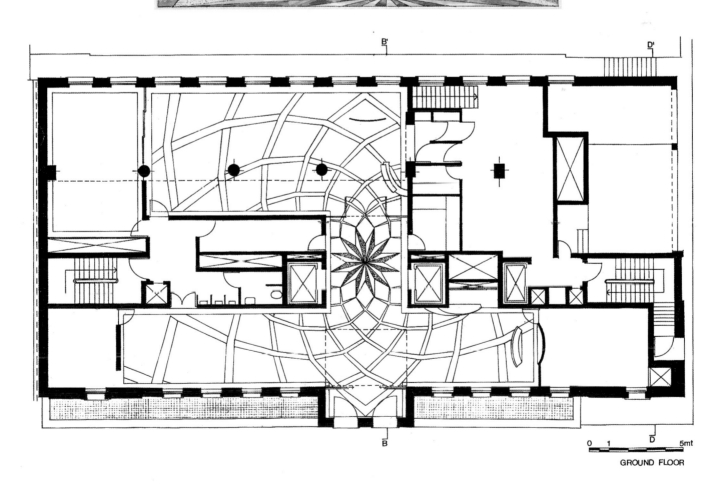

Lobby/restaurant drawing and ground floor plan.

0   1   5mt

GROUND FLOOR

*Rooms are dominated
by black, white and
creams combined with
the rosewood
panelling.*

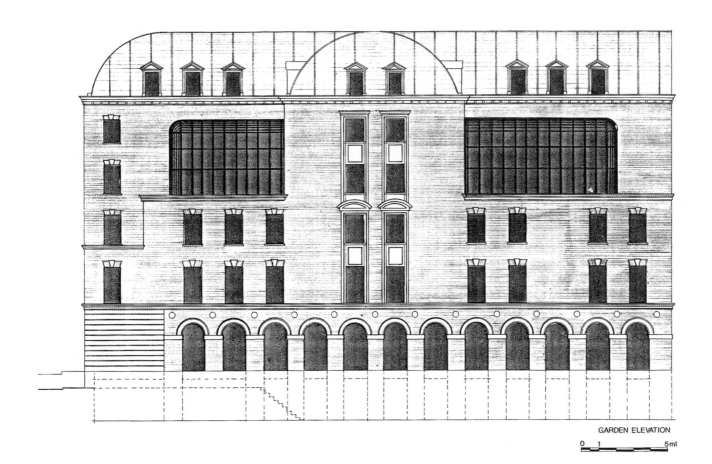

GARDEN ELEVATION

0 1   5mt

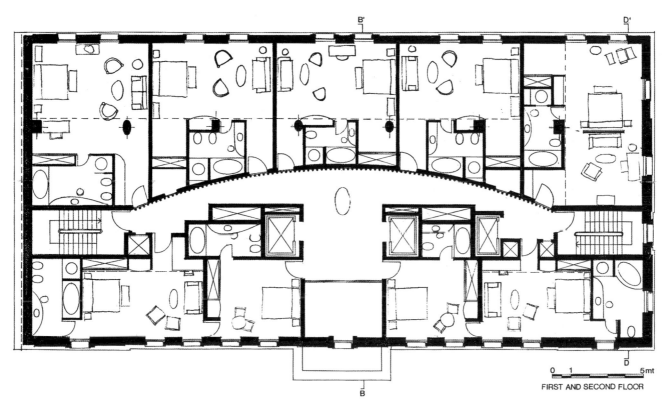

B'   D'

B   D

0 1   5mt

FIRST AND SECOND FLOOR

HOTEL SQUARE, Paris

Interior design: PATRICK DERDERIAN   1997   22 rooms   3 floors

'The hotel's passwords are calm and relaxation'

Behind the Indian green granite facade, Hotel Square offers modern charm in a relaxed contemporary setting with custom designed furniture and numerous art works.

The atrium lobby is illuminated with natural light and the main focus – the reception area – features rosewood desks and leather chairs, bronze table lamps and a distinctive scarlet coloured sofa. The floor features a square design, and the hotel's motif, which is echoed throughout the hotel in smaller form in different pigments and with the use of gold leaf. At the rear of the lobby a central structure hosts an 18 metre high hanging gallery, totalling 200 sq metres of space for artworks. Combined with the Salon Blanc on the first floor, the hotel acts as a worthy exhibition space for shows.

The lounge, located in the basement, provides a comfortable and relaxing space with an assortment of leather Chesterfields to lounge on. Walls are a deep blue in contrast to the tanned leather. Each bedroom is unique in design and boasts its own carved marble bathroom. The pin-striped bed linen and curtain hangs give a slightly executive feel to the clean lines of the rooms. Natural fibres, tones of ivory and grey, brick and saffron, gold and bronze, are the colours that pervade throughout the hotel

Perhaps most notable of all is the restaurant Zebra Square which preceded the hotel in 1995 and is one of Paris' modern brasseries. The interior has loft-like dimensions with dozens of hanging lamps, is bathed in soft woods, and seats 160 people. Situated opposite the Paris Maison de la Radio, the brasserie attracts a high profile of radio and television personalities.

The lounge features rosewood tables and leather Chesterfields. Stools are covered in mauve creating a warm and cosy atmosphere.

In contrast Salon Blanc on the first floor uses rich reds and terracotta colours to warm the white gallery space.

Ground floor plan.

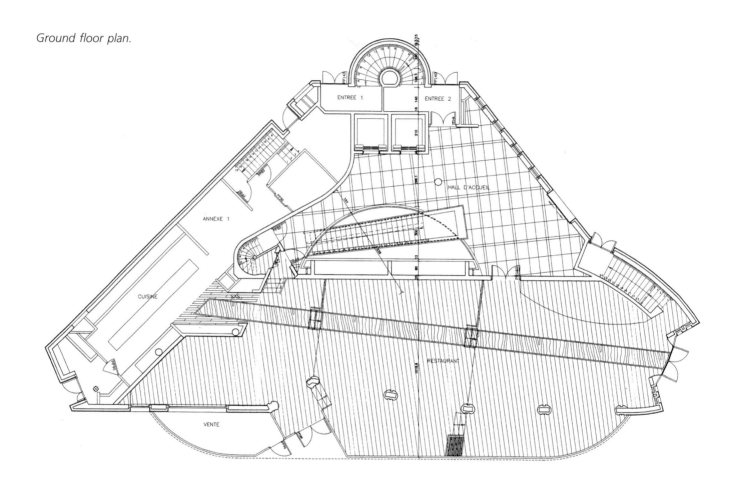

Second floor plan.

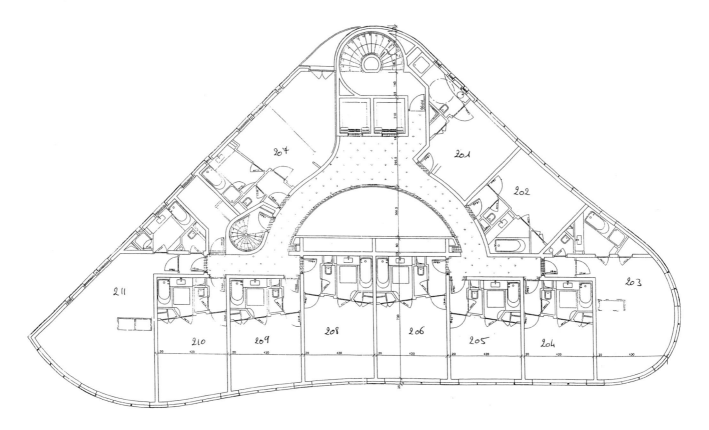

The restaurant Zebra Square with its loft-like
dimensions and hanging lamps uses soft woods and
leather upholstery.

The use of pin-stripe on the bed linen and drapes give the bedrooms a slightly executive but very clean-lined look. Bathrooms use blue marbles; the bedrooms pin-stripe is reflected in the blinds.

hotel as theatre
The Schrager/Starck Signature

The Schrager/Starck team has revolutionised hotel interiors at an international level and has pioneered a new discipline based on the experience, rather than just the look, of interiors.

Their names are now associated with unique concepts in hotel design that hover around the theme of 'hotel as theatre' where the quality of the hotel experience as a whole surpassses the appearance of the actual space and the contributions of its individual components. Themes are consistent and run through public and private spaces, so much so that as a guest you feel part of the 'party set'.

Famed hotelier Ian Schrager has introduced a philosophy for hotels as places to enjoy rather than simply places to rest your head, giving his designers freedom to create. In response, interior designer Philippe Starck has introduced a new vocabulary of spaces, challenging traditional uses and definitions, punctuating them with fun details and party-like surprises.

The Schrager/Starck team that has created 'hotel as theatre' across the globe became an internationally established signature for the late '90s stylish, sometimes bizarre, but distinctly unique, hotel interior experience. They have reinvented the lobby through Alice in Wonderland type design features, giving rise to a new 'lobby culture' for urban hotels, frequented by locals and guests alike.

Bringing glamour and make-believe into hotel design, the designs are closer to a theatrical set than typical hotel interiors, based on themes that run from the front door through the threads of the carpet, right down to the goodies in the mini-bar of each room. And it is an ever changing set – from the boutique, through cheap chic, urban resort, to the visceral experiences that a hotel can provoke.

Witty and provocative, but charming, the hotel is as much an experience as it is a place to stay.

The hotels

Ian Schrager made his name as a hotelier in New York in 1984 with Morgans on Madison Avenue, its interior designs by Parisian interior designer Andrée Putman. The hotel revolutionised the industry with the introduction of the 'boutique hotel' characterised by a consistent attention to detail throughout, giving a sense of timelessness to the designs.

The 'boutique' theme was adopted more prominently in 1987 in the first collaboration with interior designer Philippe Starck at the Royalton Hotel, New York.

Next came 'Cheap Chic' with the Paramount located in the heart of New York's theatre land. Affordable luxury offered in a cool and sophisticated environment. Lobby socialising was introduced so the hotel lobby became an important social gathering place for hotel guests and New York City dwellers alike.

Delano opened in 1995 on Miami beach presenting the notion of 'urban resort' and incorporating the idea of outdoor/indoor lobby and striking the balance between serene elegance and upbeat design.

The year 1996 saw the opening of Mondrian in Los Angeles on Sunset Boulevard, reflecting more closely the local laid-back context but combined with magic, glamour and excitement.

The manipulation of scale, and the careful balance between the extremes of magic design tricks and soothing spaces seem, however, to have reached their peak in their most recent of projects. The Schrager/Starck team crossed the Atlantic and opened St Martins Lane in central London in September 1999.

MORGANS, New York

Interior design: ANDRÉE PUTMAN

1983   112 rooms   8 floors

'The handsomest hotel in New York'

The earliest of Schragers experiments in hotel design that carved his niche and made a serious dent into conventional hotel design concepts, Morgans can be considered the first real 'design hotel' and hit the market in 1983.

With a successful history in night-club ownership, Ian Schrager and Steve Rubell turned this run-down hotel on Madison Avenue, New York, upside down. They commissioned Parisian interior designer Andrée Putman to challenge the clichés of hotel interior design and come up with something that would appeal to the design-aware market.

Putman's ideas reinvented classical designs in a creative way, playing on a black and white chequerboard graphic as a theme that runs throughout.

Entering from Madison Avenue, the lobby immediately strikes the guest as a wonderful play on Esher-style spatial shift perception with its black, grey and ecru carpet stretching wall to wall. Lighting is subdued with back-lit frosted glass panelling framed by Art Deco bronze designs and table lamps next to tan-coloured comfortable leather armchairs.

The bar in the basement features a room-length wooden table with an assortment of drum-styled African wooden stools.

Window niches afford comfortable seating spaces in each of the 112 rooms and textured walls cushion these tidy spaces with warmth. Colours are subdued and the chequerboard pattern continues through linens, shades and accessories.

PARAMOUNT, New York

1990   610 rooms

**'The Paramount's hip mix of high
design and low prices put
the typical guest room to shame.'**

In the heart of New York's theatre district, just
off Times Square, Paramount opened its own
theatrical doors in 1990. The hotel's designs
sparked off another hotel design trend known as
'cheap chic' – affordable luxury offering great
value in a cool and trendy environment. Witty
and whimsical, charming and elegant, but also at
the cutting edge of design, the Paramount
attracted local New Yorkers as well as hotel
guests to populate the 'lobby life'.

Paramount has since been updated, in 1998,
moving from 'cheap chic' to what Schrager calls
the 'urban oasis', an island of luxury in the heart
of the city. The spirit and magical essence of the
original hotel designs have been carefully
preserved but with a little more emphasis on
cosy and plush elements.

*The two-storey high lobby is the spatial and design focal point for the hotel. Tall but
inviting the space hosts a scattering of custom-made or Starck-selected furniture including
oversized mahogany sofas and long custom benches that cut dramatically through the
lobby centre. There are also designs by international artists – an armchair carved from a
single piece of wood from Swiss sculptor Natanel Gluska, and 1950s chairs by Mollino,
Albini and Zanuso. Jasper Morrison's metal 'Thinking Man's Chair', Marc Newson's
aluminium couch, and some pieces of Gaudi still remain from the original lobby. The
staircase that sweeps into the lobby from the restaurant gallery is perhaps the true focus
of the space, enhanced by a theatrical light installation that is programmed to change
throughout the day.*

The Library Bar on the mezzanine presents an alternative mood to the lobby it casts its eyes over. Cosy and comfortable, with warm lighting and a zinc-topped mahogany floating bar, the bar is lined with shelves of books giving it more of a drawing room feel.

The 610 rooms boast a 'modern minimalist sensibility' with white linens, soft lighting and, for some, dramatic headboards. These rooms' famed headboards feature gilt framed images of the 17th century master Vermeer.

ROYALTON, New York

1988   205 rooms

'spectacular'

Schrager's second 'boutique hotel' was to mark the beginning of a series of creative collaborations with French designer Philippe Starck, bringing to the otherwise static hospitality industry a completely new and original interpretation of interior hotel spaces, functions and furnishings.

Housed in the original Hotel Royalton built in 1898, Schrager's completely renovated Royalton opened its theatrical doors in mid Manhattan, New York, in 1988.

Playing on the 'home-away-from-home' theme, the Royalton was created as a 'mansion-hotel' complete with a living room, dining room, library, kitchen, breakfast room and recreation area on the ground floor, with bedrooms upstairs. With a clubby type atmosphere, more than ten years on the Royalton still retains an air of New York groove.

The very classical facade and entrance from the original building of 1898.

The multi-level lobby takes centre stage as the first step in 'hotel as theatre' concept, full of surprise details and hidden functions but also very cosy. The path is led by a dramatic blue carpet with the Starcks' decorative yellow signature, also known as the lobby 'catwalk' for those who wish to participate. Check-in desks, elevators and bathrooms are all concealed from view and must be dug out.

Off the main lobby area are the leather clad Round Bar, shaped as its name and accommodating just 20 guests and their champagne glasses; the Sunken Study, which parades as a 20ft long library table with its collection of books; a Games Room; Sushi Bar; and the all-American '44' restaurant.

Oversized rooms and suites separate areas for working, sleeping, entertaining and bathing and 40 of the 205 rooms have working fireplaces.

Bathrooms feature custom built 5ft wide round tubs and stainless steel sinks.

DELANO, Miami

1995   238 rooms

'America's coolest hotel'

Known as the 'urban resort on Miami beach' when it first opened in 1995, Delano has since been refitted in 1998, expanding its original concepts to the edge of the Atlantic Ocean.

This European style, private 'beach village' combines Italian Amalfi coast romance, Greek exoticism and local Miami beach culture to create an open-air enclave made up of tents, cabanas and a 40ft pastel striped lighthouse – the 'welcome beacon'.

The indoor/outdoor lobby consists of nine distinct areas that together aim to 'offer a seamless separation between the indoors and the outdoors'. It includes the Rose Bar with rose coloured walls and a floating bar; six different indoor/outdoor eateries; a vast collection of international furniture; and landscaped gardens or 'The Orchard' with a series of marble picnic tables and antique metal beds to lounge on. The pool has been reconnected as the 'water salon' with underwater music and water furniture to amuse.

The Blue Door restaurant is slightly more formal in design with low marble tables and comfortable leather chairs. The Blue Door Brasserie, however, hosts a typically Starck styled 15ft long bar and 12ft panelled screen comprised of hand etched Venetian mirrors.

Rooms are a variety of lofts, suites and poolside bungalows with the accent on 'barefoot chic'. Custom-painted white and pearl grey, with mirror-glazed brilliant white wide-plank wood floors, the rooms pride themselves on their pristine and tranquil decor. Modern simplicity for the cool barefoot Miami babe . . .

Bathrooms are luxurious with floor to ceiling seamless slabs of thick Italian arabescato marble recalling the baths of ancient Rome.

The beach is decorated with a series of
coloured tents and cabanas, with a
stripy 'welcome beacon' in the middle.

MONDRIAN, Los Angeles

1996   238 rooms   12 floors

'An elegant masterpiece'

Part of a collection of 36 bar stools representing an assortment of design styles in the Lobby Table.

In his fourth collaboration with Starck, Schrager aimed to repackage the traditional notion of Hollywood glamour and modernise it.

Set in sunny California the 12 storey 238 suite Mondrian prides itself on bridging the gap between the casual-outdoors-easy-living-culture and a more upbeat-glamorous-Los Angeles city sensibility. Introducing the idea of 'uncomplicated sophistication', the overtly stereotypical superficial glamour usually associated with Hollywood has been thrown out, and replaced with more gracious and elegant design, but with the usual razor-sharp Starck finish to it.

The Lobby Table reinterprets the traditional function of a diner, coffee shop and bar all in one, creating more a Family Table with varied uses through the day and night and surrounded by a collection of 36 bar stools representing an assortment of design styles. In addition there are more than 200 pieces of furniture and objects by named designers, part of Starck's international flea-market collection.

The Sky Bar is a simple tin-roofed open-air hut supported by logs with panoramic views across LA and furnished with wood pieces in a traditional American schoolhouse style.

Light installations throughout are by renowned artist James Turrell.

The indoor/outdoor lobby in Mondrian magically transports the outdoors in and the indoors out. A borderless and flowing space is created using layers of curtains and luminescent walls inside the 30ft mahogany entrance doors. Natural sky-colours with bursts of acid-bright hues are employed in an attempt to blur the distinction between reality and illusion.

Rooms are simple but full of surprises. Most have floor-to-ceiling glass walls to 'bring the outside in' and are laid out much like a home – with living room, kitchen, work area and bedroom as divided spaces, their furnishings spare but elegant.

ST MARTINS LANE, London

1999   204 rooms   7 floors

**'an utterly original urban resort in this
most international of cities'**

On seven storeys in the heart of London's Covent
Garden, St Martins Lane with its 204 rooms is
the latest completed project designed by Philippe
Starck for Ian Schrager. Magical, flooded with
light, and full of bizarre objects on an Alice in
Wonderland scale – with gold teeth as stools and
outsized yellow revolving doors – the lobby, as
centre stage, is an experience in its own right –
'a triumph of colour and light'. Lobby culture.
Grand station concourse. Bedrooms behind the
scenes. Full of secrets – room numbers picked
out on the carpet; red light on the door knob
means vacant and green means engaged. Drama
in the corridors with different coloured doorways.

The lobby as the main stage, all lights and action, with yellow curved walls and a bizarre collection of eclectic furniture – from a Salvador Dali 'Leda' cast-bronze arm chair to gold leaf molar-teeth stools.

Clean white rooms, more like booths, give a certain sumptuous and calm touch away from the excitement of the lobby and restaurants. Each room boasts floor-to-ceiling windows, pristine white linen, Venetian blinds and terracotta pots mounted on the wall. But perhaps the most notable fun feature is the light by the bed which can be customised to any colour of the rainbow resulting in a colourful grid of lights from the street.

Saint M restaurant is a modern twist on a classic brasserie. Comfortably plush with more traditional dark wood themes, dark wood tables, mirrored central bar, exotic African wood panelling and pure white marble floors.

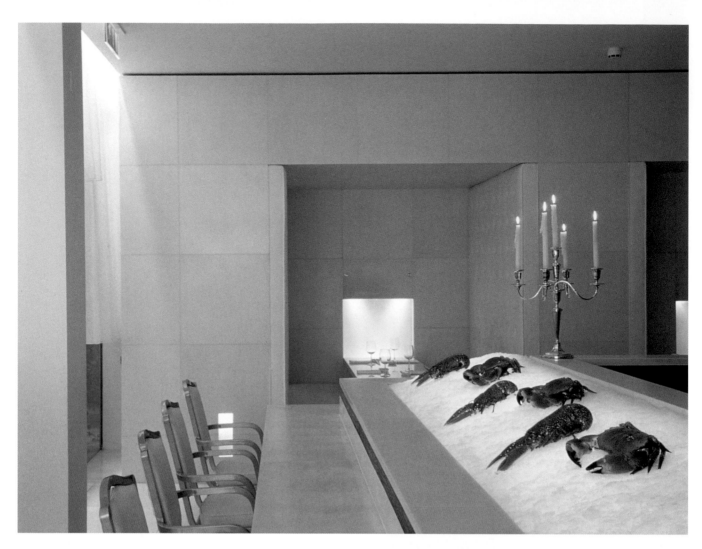

The Sea Bar, inspired by local fish markets, and constructed from seamless marble and mounds of ice. Patrons sit around the luminescent bar on custom designed Louis XVI style aluminium chairs that are all white upholstered.

But perhaps the most notable fun feature is the light by the bed which can be customised to any colour of the rainbow resulting in a colourful grid of lights reflecting on to the street.

Asia de Cuba. A mix of majestic 'art columns' run through this restaurant, offering different artistic applications. All column installations change regularly to showcase the work of guest artists. Furniture is simple and elegant, brushed aluminium, yellow glass and light boxes glowing with yellow tulips.

Light Bar. Atmospheric and interactive lighting, changing from night to day. The ceiling features voids that cast shafts of purple, green, yellow and red down upon Starck's pristine white communal drinking table.

Branding the boutique

The W chain

Introduction

The W Group in New York, Atlanta, San Francisco, Seattle.

Seeing a gap in the market for a 'fun, hip and exciting hotel collection that happily marries boutique hotel flair with the quality and functionality of larger brand hotels', Starwood Hotels and Resorts Worldwide Inc. have invented a new brand of hotel called simply W. (Starwood Hotels and Resorts Worldwide Inc. own a variety of internationally recognised hotel brands including Sheraton, Westin, Caesars and The St Regis/Luxury Collection.)

W is the first boutique-style chain to be established in the hotel industry and carves its own niche among its sister brands of the Westin, Sheraton and Luxury Collection. Self-labelled as lifestyle hotels, W try to reflect what is popular in contemporary home furnishings. The designers' brief for W hotels has been to design a hotel that is fashionable in home interiors today but to add elements of fun and surprise. Each hotel is commissioned from different architects and interior designers, but is conceived in collaboration with the Starwood Design team, headed by Theresa Fatino.

Heralded as the 'unique union of style and substance', W hotels are appearing in all major cities across America, priding themselves on their reliability (in terms of traditional hotel functions) but combined with 'hip', 'chic' and 'boutique' labels. Fully comprehensive business facilities and hip design synthesise to produce the chained 'style' hotel.

This new boutique-style chain supported by a well established international system of sales, reservations and frequent stay programmes, will eventually consist of 16 hotels building a portfolio of W hotels throughout the US. (W hotel's 'w' stands for Warmth, Witty, Wonderful and Welcoming and originated from Starwood's President and CEO Berry Sternlicht.)

Presented here are the first of their W hotels in New York, Atlanta, San Francisco and Seattle.

W NEW YORK,
The organic trial

Interior design: DAVID ROCKWELL OF ROCKWELL GROUP

1998   722 rooms   7 floors

The first of the W hotels which opened in
December 1998 was designed by David Rockwell,
already renowned for his innovative interior
design work for restaurants, and located in the
heart of central Manhattan, New York City. This
1928 building on the corner of Lexington Avenue
and 49th Street was completely transformed into
a haven of minimalist lines, natural light and
earthy colours.

A modern and 'funky' environment with
trendy bars and functional conference rooms, the
hotel has been given the 'organic' treatment:
wheatgrass can be found growing out of seating
in public areas; dried fruits and vegetables
texture the check-in desk backdrop; dried leaves
are pressed in glass panels, tree stumps are used
as chess boards, and natural fabrics are to be
found throughout. The check-in desk is set
against the 'Garden Wall' – a cubist collage of
seeds, dried flowers and grasses, shells, leaves
and stones; and for continuity, wheatgrass can
be bought in pots at the magazine stand or in
liquid form as wheatgrass juice at the juice bar.

The lobby lounge, an open space two storeys high, faces on to 49th Street through the coloured glass window panels. There is an assortment of comfortable sofas and cushioned stools with tree stumps as game boards. Organic flower displays decorate bars and tables.

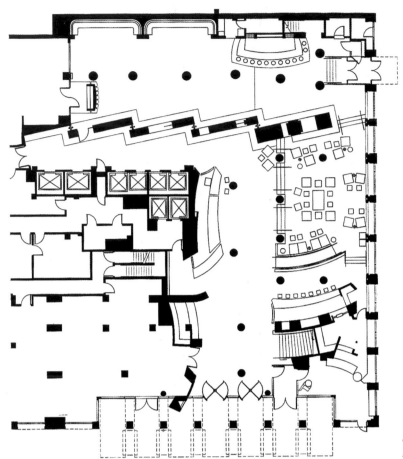

Ground floor plan. The street entrance is shown at the bottom edge.

Whiskey Bar Blue bar on the ground floor comprises soft velvet cushions and covers and cool black and white photographs of New York City. In the middle of the bar floor is a bed for public lounging with deep sensual-coloured velvet bed throws.

A waterfall cascades down a glass wall in the middle dividing the lounge from the Heartbeat restaurant, which itself is full of healthy organic drapes and icons. The round columns are brightly decorated with glass mosaics while other columns are draped in silks and lit from behind, adding a flutter of movement to the scene as people pass. Heartbeat restaurant, which features organic food and healthy menus, is run by restaurateur Drew Nieporent of Nobu, Montrachet and others and famed in New York for his excellent taste and eateries.

The 722 plush rooms feature oversized desks, luxuriously big beds, and all mod cons for the business traveller wrapped up in 'organic' tones, natural fabrics and Aveda products. Single rooms are tight on space at 280 sq ft but feature unusual headboard cut-outs and silk-screened soundbites on the bed linen reading 'Walk with Confidence' or 'Sleep with Angels'. The bedding is also available for purchase.

W ATLANTA

Architect:
CELESTE BECKER FOR CW DESIGN

Minimalist lines and natural woods dominate W Atlanta.

Soft fabrics in ecru and white are used throughout bars and restaurants.

Rooms are comfortable and plush with strong blues and reds in contrast to natural woods and light linens.

W SAN FRANCISCO

Architects:
HORNBERGER & WORSTELL

Interior design: SHOPWORKS, LLC. AND PARSONS DESIGN

The lobby and adjoining lounge are dominated by the two storey centrepiece, with its patterned stone floors contrasting with the tan coloured leather seating. Solid warm tones dot the scene with yellows, lilacs, blues and reds on softer deeper brown sofas.

Chrome, wood and egg lights
lead the bar's theme.

Rooms are unfussy and
comfortable with solid
coloured bed throws and
natural mushroom fabrics.

W SEATTLE

Architects and interior designers:
CALLISON ARCHITECTURE, INC.

W Seattle bar/restaurant

OPPOSITE: Exterior night shot of W Seattle occupying the lower floors of the building.

The lobby lounge features a bold blue stripey wall, yellow rings and curves, and an assortment of dark, comfortable furniture.

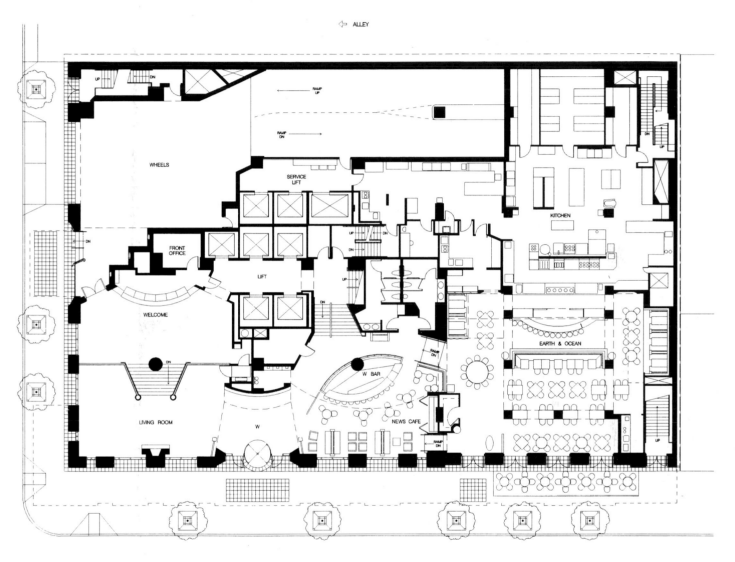

First floor plan.

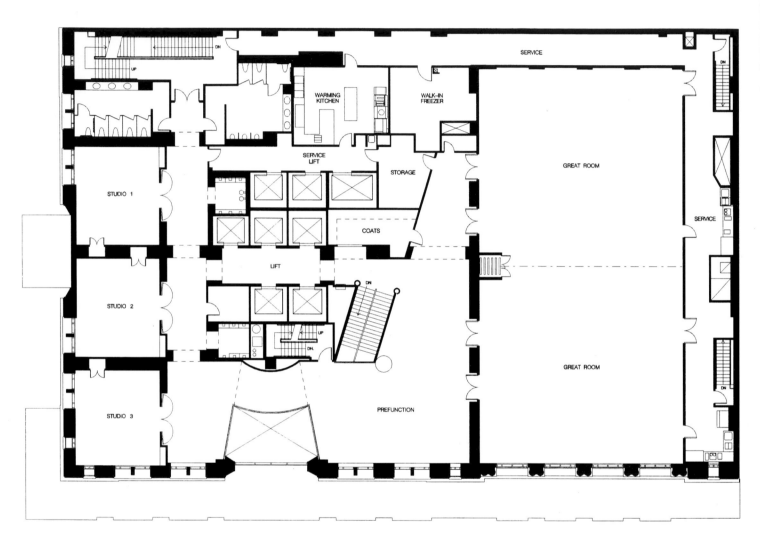

Second floor plan.

Rooms are minimal in mushroom and taupe colours and solid blue fabrics; bathrooms feature long glass tops and steel sinks.

hybrids

The chapter on Hybrids presents three examples in which a non-interior designer has been asked to develop the interior designs of a hotel. The three projects are different in all respects but for this common idea. The work of fashion designers, which is very much textile led, and a film set designer, whose work resembles more a series of sets for scenes, is showcased here in very different settings with very different outcomes.

Perhaps this crossing-over of design represents the way forward for hoteliers looking for a non-typical and non-brand approach to hotel design.

THE STANDARD, Los Angeles

Interior design: SHAWN HAUSMAN

140 rooms   1999

'Pop sensibility of the 50s, 60s and 70s that add up to 2000'

Sister to the Mercer, New York, over on the East Coast, the Standard, LA, is owned by Andre Balazs and shares the same sensibility of cool comfort and hip luxury, but with an affordable-playful 1970s sci-fi approach. To revamp this wavy-balconied 1964 motel, which had also done time as a retirement home, Balazs called in designers Newson (furniture) and Hausman (film production and set designer) to transform and delight. Electric blue Astro-Turf cools the sun deck and surrounds the pool, shag-pile carpet warms the lobby floor and ceiling, and silver bean bag chairs decorate rooms. An Austin Powers dream hotel.

A row of potted cacti in the lobby which also features shag-pile carpets and a performance art space with resident DJ spinning ambient sounds.

The Smurf-blue Astro-Turf that surrounds the swimming pool.

*Curtains are patterned
with a mid 1960s
Andy Warhol print.*

Beds are inspired by the Gio Ponte design, rooms are home to silver bean bag chairs, Eamesian surfboard tables, inflatable chairs from IKEA, and fun phones. Mini-bars are reportedly stocked with a colourful assortment of condoms.

THE MORRISON, Dublin

Architects and interior designers: DOUGLAS | WALLACE

Design consultant: JOHN ROCHA

1999   94 rooms   5 floors

'the perfect expression of the new Dublin'

The Morrison Hotel on Ormond Quay, Dublin makes a confident statement as a building in terms of height, rhythm and the palette of materials. Created by Douglas | Wallace, the interior unfolds revealing a series of interlocking volumes from reception into the double-height restaurant and lounges. The spaces are defined by a diagonal wall which permeates every public area.

John Rocha, the internationally acclaimed fashion designer who has lived in Ireland for 21 years, acted as a design consultant. He explains: 'The client's brief was to create a hotel that was primarily Irish but also complementary to current contemporary lifestyle, and incorporating Oriental influences.

'Modern design is about mixing designs and in the Morrison I have tried to mix the Oriental with local design. For example, we have used local artists to paint the 140 paintings for each space and room as well as sourcing artefacts from the East. The fabrics too are hand painted and the sculptures commissioned.

'It is not about making a grand statement but rather about making both the local person and the international traveller feel at home.'

Lush, sensual and Irish, the Morrison is a mix of styles and spaces, and pleasant tactile surprises.

In the lobby/lounge area soft leather stools and covered sofas are made comfortable with intimate red and pink hand-painted silk velvet cushions.

The check-in desk is framed by the warm gold designs of one of the commissioned paintings. Custom made furniture is found in front by the thick columns. Tall heavy mirrors lean against the wall adding an altered perspective by tilting the reception at an angle.

The Halo, the cathedral-like restaurant, opens up
two floors of space and light soaking up the best
part of the atrium, with a theatrical-style staircase
trimming one edge of the room from the ground to
the skies. The lights, suspended above the diners,
almost resemble sea-gulls in mid-flight. The area for
food is curtained off with two vast velvet hangs,
the height of the room, weighty and serious with
religious overtones.

The two bars on the left and right off the first corridor are a mixture of wood and leather, ecru and deep brown. One is open to the pathway of guests following the line to the reception on the lower ground at the end, while the second bar is closed with more intimate corners and cosy alcoves. Shelves of bottles and glasses behind the bar are softened by leafed-paper lanterns and basket covered lights, a meeting point between the Irish pub-scene and more tranquil Oriental moments.

The club/bar in the basement is dominated by a huge gold dish hung on the back wall (by a local artist who added to an otherwise discarded satellite dish) and a sculpted head of dark wood that sits in the middle of the room, chin touching the floor and head reaching the ceiling. The room is softened with lights hidden behind baskets, red ponyskin seats, and dangly reflections from spidery lights.

The 87 rooms and 7 suites tend to accentuate the calm of the Orient with luscious velvet throws across the bed, or a lily delicately placed in a pool of water inside a crystal bowl. Walls are curved to give maximum space and to soften the otherwise usually hard edge where bedroom meets bathroom.

DWAR EL OMDA, El Gouna, Egypt

Interior design: SHAHIRA FAHMY

Lighting design: ZAKI SHERIFF

1997   66 rooms   3 floors

'a play on the traditional palace with touches of *baladi* (country)'

The Dwar El Omda literally translated means the Major's House. It is a house found commonly in the rural landscape of Upper Egypt among the *felaheen* (farmers) villages. The Dwar El Omda hotel was designed as a charming play between the traditional Islamic palace and the local kitsch '*baladi*' styles, using Arab-inspired architecture and interiors.

Incorporating aspects of Egypt's Islamic medieval heritage found in the old city of Cairo, Sheriff aimed to inspire the local community with a touch of their own style instead of importing the latest 'chic' designs from abroad, as commonly happens in new hotel designs in Egypt. The architectural proportions and spaces, rooted in the same tradition, were appropriate for developing his style of work. Huge spectacular domes can thus be seen filled with massive chandeliers that encircle the space, accentuating the heights afforded by the dome. Playing on mix of kitsch and traditional ideas, Sheriff caricatured the original designs but used space and light creatively. Perhaps the most amusing touch are the rows of nearly transparent blue glass light shades in the ground floor corridor that resemble inverted condoms.

Interior designer Shahira Fahmy, responsible primarily for colours, textiles and furnishings, took as her inspiration original mayors' houses around Upper Egypt.

Fahmy sourced textiles and furniture from all over Egypt – from the backstreet markets in Cairo to disused and half-demolished houses in Upper Egyptian villages. The results of her searches can be seen throughout the hotel as an eclectic collection of doors, urns, picture frames, huge chests and various bits of typical *felaheen* furniture.

The lobby entrance is framed by two huge impressive doors, inside of which a line of water pitchers sits at eye level, a symbolic gesture of the freely offered communal thirst quencher on hot summer days.

Above the check-in desk sits a tattered, old but amusing portrait of an Omda (a mayor) with his stern authoritative gaze and the heavy look of a country man.

The Istanbul style divans found throughout the public spaces of the hotel give extra seating depth than normal Western couches, and in typical Middle Eastern style allow the sitter to be cross-legged while leaning on a central cushion. An assortment of small usually brass 'chi' tables from which to take the tea customarily offered on arrival are always at hand. The floor pattern throughout the Dwar, best seen in the courtyard, is one of vine and geometric flower patterns in pastel reds, yellows and greens inspired by the floors of existing Dwars.

On the first floor is a public area of brightly coloured divans
and kitsch baladi textiles. Fuchsia, orange and gold cushions
pad the tall brass beds in a style typical of a country girl's
wedding dowry, equipped with a small clumsily decorated
box that would hold the bride's belongings. The chandelier
hangs with naked bulbs – typical of country houses.

En route to the restaurant an unusual tea room is situated
on its own with a round but low table decorated with tea
pots and ornate trays. Walls are terracotta reds with gold
stencilled designs and the doorway is masked with strings of
gold beading.

The restaurant itself, which overlooks the courtyard, is a series of three rooms, each dominated by a dome in which hangs a huge chandelier either of hand blown blue glass shades or of more Syrian inspired iron based designs.

The courtyard that opens on to a small swimming pool and an additional section of the hotel is decorated above with strings of filigree lights and on the ground with a variety of larger local artefacts, mainly urns and water pitchers.

new for old: adaptive re-use

In this chapter three projects are presented which have all adapted an old building into a new hotel. The original function of the building – in these cases a prison, a convent and a car factory – can often dominate the overall interior architecture of the building, giving the interiors a ready-made identity. It is the job of the interior architect and designer to adapt these historical characteristics in such a way as to complement their new contemporary designs while holding on to some of the building's original identity.

In the case of Istanbul's prison and Milan's convent, where both adaptations were executed by Four Seasons, new interior designs are explicitly woven around the existing interiors, highlighting the history – for example, original frescoes are left untouched in the lobby and lounge, and room layout is more or less as the original.

In contrast is Renzo Piano's creative mixed-use solution for Turin's old Fiat car factory, that includes in part a business-oriented hotel managed by Le Meridien. The shell of the factory building remains while all interiors have been completely redesigned, and to keep the history of the conversion alive many sketches, drawings, plans and photographs of the old becoming the new are placed in the interiors. Contemporary furnishings and materials are used throughout giving a very strong modern signature to some of the larger spaces that clearly derive from another building type.

FOUR SEASONS, Istanbul

Interior design: SINAN KAFADAR, METEX DESIGN GROUP

1996   65 rooms   converted prison

'Classic luxury in an authentic historical setting'

This four-storey building of 1917 is a wonderful example of late Ottoman/early Turkish neo-classical architecture and has been designated a historic treasure. Originally a prison that once housed dissident artists, writers and philosophers, its thick walls have been adapted and restored as a hotel, taking great care not to alter dramatically the historic fabric of the building.

Though an upper-class international hotel, the building stands today as a 'celebration of artistic endeavour in honour of the many famous writers, artists and scholars who were incarcerated there during the days of oppression' and is perfectly located in the vicinity of some of the city's great architectural landmarks, namely the Hagia Sophia and the Blue Mosque.

Set around an open courtyard, the designs and furnishings of this conversion draw on Turkish culture and the region's oriental heritage, specifically late Ottoman designs.

The exterior walls have carefully preserved the original decorative tiling while glass additions connect the original buildings and frame the inner courtyard, affording more natural light to the interiors. Original high ceilings and expansive windows dominate the interior architecture giving an interesting variety of shapes and sizes of rooms and public spaces, the majority of rooms (though not all) being left unchanged from their original arrangement. Materials comprise marble, mosaics, wood, wrought iron, while floor patterns draw on traditional oriental geometric designs. Small oriental details decorate throughout in the form of discreet wood carvings on the furniture, kilims and other carpets, and the rich assortment of antique Islamic artefacts.

The arched main entrance with original 1917 facade details.

The lobby's uncluttered and simple arched architecture connects the bar, lobby and reception areas. Chairs, sofas and tables are modern interpretations of traditional oriental designs with a variety of Turkish wrought iron artefacts.

The impressive courtyard also details a colourful blend of Ottoman tiles, marble, greenery and bird cages, and acts as the hotel's visual and focal centre. The inner courtyard contains one of the hotel's more internationally styled restaurants, housed in a glass enclosure with an outdoor terrace attached.

In a two storey suite, the oak timbers from the old prison structure were used to reinforce the roof. The headboard and bed posts draw on domes and minarets.

FOUR SEASONS, Milan

Interior design: PAMELA BABEY OF BABEY-MOULTON JUE AND BOOTH
1993   98 rooms   3 floors   Restored 15th century convent

'more like an intimate palazzo than a hotel'

Located in Milan's famous golden triangle between Via Monte Napoleone, Via della Spiga and Sant 'Andrea, the entrance to the Four Seasons Milano is actually tucked away discreetly on Via Gesú. Housed in a restored 15th century convent the hotel has managed to recover much of the building's original interior architecture – the courtyard, cloisters, columns, fresco decorated vaults – and has carefully integrated them, in a three and a half year project, as features alongside more modern day classic design.

Interestingly it was not until the redesign of the interiors was underway that parts of the building dating back to the 15th century were discovered. Frescoes had been buried beneath layers of plaster, vaulted ceilings hidden behind masonry. The relevant authorities were called in to declare these fragments national monuments thus adding a further 18 months to the design schedule. Today, above the concierge's desk, one can see a portion of a fresco thought to depict the story of the Adoration of Jesus by the Three Wise Men with one of the magi still visible; even some suites and rooms reveal their original vaulted ceilings.

However, the modern interior designs do not try to recreate or copy the original life of the building but rather allow the original remnants to stand alongside the modern contemporary lines, low furniture, light colours, lights and furnishings. The result is a calm but layered mix of the historic and the contemporary.

The lobby and lounge, which was originally the chapel, was not altered spatially. The four ancient columns, ceiling vaults and arched walls that were all uncovered remain intact. Fresco fragments were cleaned. Walls are a mixture of plaster and pulverised marble giving a finish very close to the original. Original remnants now stand alongside the modern contemporary lines, low furniture, light colours, lights and furnishings. The foyer bar also features 19th century drawings of stage sets for operas and ballets by Filippo Peroni who was La Scala's chief set designer for 18 years.

The white spiral staircase was an addition in the architectural restructuring.

The wonderfully expansive courtyard and cloisters have been retained and galleries enclosed with glass.

A sunken court in the middle of the garden lights up the basement restaurant and other adjoining rooms.

Bedrooms also feature
vaulted and decorated
ceilings with classic
luxurious furnishings.
Colours are warm with
shades of celadon, gold or
terracotta. Bathrooms are
marble with deep whirlpool
tubs.

LE MÉRIDIEN LINGOTTO, Turin

Interior architecture: RENZO PIANO BUILDING WORKSHOP

Interior design: FRANCO MIRENZI, UNIMARK

1995   224 rooms   Two 3 floor wings   Converted Fiat car factory

'one of the most spectacular examples of 1920s industrial architecture . . . ideal to welcome the most distinguished guest'

Le Méridien Lingotto is housed in an 80 year old monumental factory building whose many functions and uses are still being defined and developed. Originally a Futurist building from the 1920s it was built by architect Giacomo Matte-Trucco for the legendary Fiat car factory in Turin, northern Italy. Car assembly would begin on the ground floor and continue up until it reached the infamous test-track on the roof (later to be featured in the 1960s film *The Italian Job* starring Michael Caine and Mini cars).

The conversion of this monument was won by competition in the late 1980s by Italian architect Renzo Piano who presented a 'city within a city' as the design solution, including concert hall, shopping street, the bubble (an extraordinary conference room), piazzas, and Le Méridien Lingotto hotel.

The 224 room Lingotto hotel comprises two of the three storey wings within the entire factory complex, which are connected by a glass walled tunnel that cuts through the 'Garden of Wonders' – an internal courtyard planted with subtropical greenery. Interior designs complement the original life of the building, but without the industrial edge. Colours are neutral sitting with the warm and bold, contemporary furniture of Italian design, and public spaces vast and expansive, calmed by the extensive use of greenery. However, displayed throughout the spaces are sketches and pictures of the building as it was and through its fantastical transformation, pictures that continue to remind the guest of its past.

The ground floor houses a vast open lobby/lounge with 9 metre high ceilings, tall plants and floor-to-ceiling glass windows that overlook the green courtyard. Adjoining are the restaurant and bar – a conversion of the original cafeteria for the 'operai' – and corridors leading to an exhibition centre. The lobby walls are decorated with the original competition entries for the transformation of the factory for mixed use. Furniture is low and contemporary, sitting on oriental carpets and kilims, colours neutral with raw woods.

The glass corridor that links the two wings cutting through the courtyard, the 'Garden of Wonders'.

The lobby area outside the elevators on each floor displays a fantastic oversized technical sketch on blue background by the Renzo Piano Building Workshop demonstrating some aspect of the building's conversion. Wire backed chairs that circle the low table are covered in contrast with a warm solid red fabric.

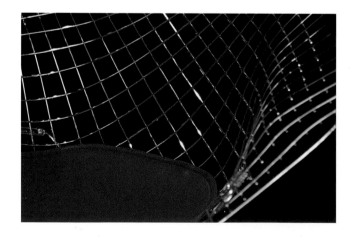

The rooms, on three floors, are regular in shape and host a variety of contemporary chairs and sofas in solid reds, oranges, blues and deep red leather, and desks in light wood. Pencil and ink sketches relating to the building decorate the walls.

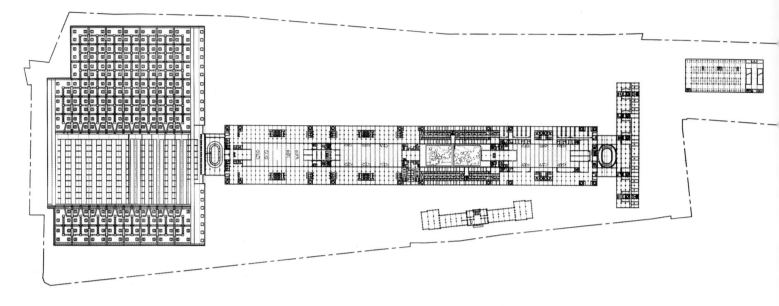

Ground floor plan.

The ramp to bring the car back down to the ground floor and out of the building is perhaps the most spectacular piece of architectural Futurist work in the Lingotto.

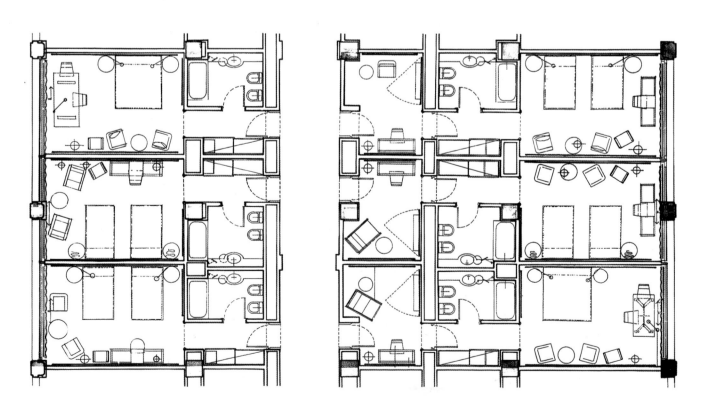

Typical room plans.

External elevation.

The 'bubble' conference centre on the roof, housed in a cantilevered High-tech structure and designed by English artist-engineer Peter Rice, can be reached by elevator from the ground floor.

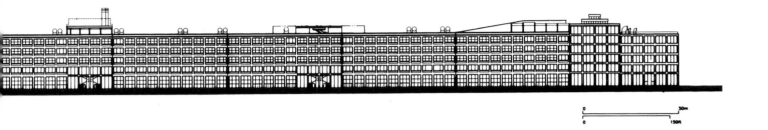

other worlds: vegas

A whole volume could easily be dedicated to the dynamics of design in the desert city of Las Vegas; it would be both fascinating, in terms of the design possibilities, and wild, in terms of scale and size of budgets. Our space is limited here to the designs of only four hotels and these four have been selected on the basis that they represent a variety in the latest philosophy (of theme-ing) and approach (in contemporary design) of Vegas hotels. However, references are given to other Vegas hotels to illustrate various points.

The city

The year 1999 saw another 20 thousand rooms added to the already existing 100 thousand rooms in the gambling mecca of Vegas (Disney resorts host an approximate 85 thousand). And another round of mega-budgets to support them: the Italian inspired Bellagio cost $1.8bn to complete; the Venetian $1bn; the Paris $780m; the new Aladdin $1.5bn.

These 3000 room hotels aim to deliver the service of a 300 room hotel according to one hotel manager, but it is a small wonder how this could ever be possible. Interaction between staff and guest is minimal, and other than the initial check-in when the key card is handed over there need be no more. However, Vegas is the most visited city in the world (last year's figures recorded a total of 33 million guests) and is the fastest growing city in America with an average of 7000 new people settling each month adding to the residential population of one million.

And in addition to the new mega-casino resorts that pull the crowds, fine-dining in contemporary styled restaurants with named chefs is being used as a new and successful marketing tool.

Scale

Vegas is like design on steroids. Anything designed for Vegas hotels necessitates the addition of another two or three noughts – whether to the budget, the order form for materials, or the design team.

There is a certain horror mixed with fascination at the sheer scale of all these projects. Most hotels in Vegas can accommodate between 2000–3000 guests (the MGM tops this at 5000) which makes the job of the designer and his team a far cry from what is needed in terms of design considerations for a hotel in a European city, for example.

Check-in desks are on a par with an airport check-in arrangement with areas divided by ropes and information displayed above each desk; and lobbies are vast spaces that merge into the casino floor or spill into mega shopping malls. The hotel is big enough to become another world, and by shutting out daylight and denying any measure of natural time, it encourages the guest to forget his normal daily reality.

Replicature

Vegas is one big 'design laboratory' where designers and architects are allowed to push themes to extremes and design to excess. The term 'replicature' is knocked around this desert town referring to the various hotel structures that seek literally to replicate that which they refer to, rather than making more discreet design reference to.

The Venetian Hotel and Casino, and the New York New York Hotel and Casino, are early examples of this approach where the place (in this case Venice or New York) is almost recreated in its entirety on a limited scale. The most notable city references – the canals in Venice, the skyscrapers and Brooklyn Bridge of New York – are reproduced in the middle of the electric city of gambling and showgirls.

Our most recent example – The Paris Hotel and Casino – has brought the most stereotypical symbols of Paris to Nevada in the form of an Eiffel Tower, the façades of the Opera house and the Arc de Triomphe. The interiors follow suit by recreating Paris street scenes with ceilings painted as skies, and lighting fixed at twilight 24 hours a day.

At a less literal level but creating a commotion of references, the Bellagio Hotel and Casino, which rejects the idea of 'replicature', has taken an old Italian villa from the Lake Como area as the basis for its design theme. The result is far from the style, ambience or scale of an old Italian villa, but instead overflows with luxurious details (finishing, furnishings, textiles, artworks) from all over the world and from all periods of history, including the Italian. The lobby, for example, houses an impressive contemporary glass flower sculpture suspended from the ceiling; leading on from there are the indoor gardens with the grandest of grand marble staircases; and the gaming rooms that host the most incredible collection of antique Asian art.

"The Americans wish to copy", said the manager of one of these hotels. "If we can bring it to them rather than them going there, we will! Instead of touring the world in 80 days, the American's insatiable appetite for entertainment and leisure can be satisfied within eight days. We have Paris, Venice, Lake Como, and New York all on one street!"

In contrast, the Mandalay Bay Hotel uses Asia as its theme but does not try to replicate any particular place or culture. It is perhaps the most successful in incorporating some of the more fantastic contemporary works of interior design (check its Oriel restaurant) that complement the bizarre context.

Though the Bellagio aspires to 'replicate' Italy, the Paris the real French capital, and the Venetian to recreate Venice, what you actually end up with is a distorted idea of Europe and European designs, spanning any number of centuries. The overall effect is shocking and fascinating, and also memorable. But however Eurostyle (or Eurotrash) these hotels try to be with their impressive lobbies and restaurants, sadly most of the bedrooms tend to be bland and disappointing in terms of design and could easily fit into the league of international cut-and-paste hotel design.

Navigation

These vast hotel structures with their thousands of rooms are designed to manipulate the dimensions of time (for example, the public lighting at the Paris hotel is permanently set to twilight) and to support an environment that not only entertains but also disorientates and distorts. Layout is often confusing, configured to obscure exits, and usually does not conform to any typical experience of a hotel space. The design of the gaming area serves to increase the complexity of the interiors with its never-ending barrage of light and sound. The line between lobby and gaming areas is blurred, and subsequently the lobby area has lost any sense of intimacy.

Design or direction?

Hotel design for Vegas involves a team of architects, designers, engineers, lighting designers, pyrotechnicians and water consultants.

The primary function of hotels is entertainment so designers must work with the discipline of show design in mind. This is putting entertainment before architecture and entertainment before design.

The process of design is more akin to making a film, an art form from which Vegas draws much of its inspiration. Tight teamwork is required to pull it off.

Vegas sleaze

Despite all the effort, energy and money put into new contemporary designs for these mega-hotels, the original Vegas sleaze still abounds. Vegas would not be Vegas without its shag-pile carpets, mirrored ceilings, fresco-decorated 24 hour wedding chapel, and assaulting neon from its thousands of slot machines.

The projects

Presented here are three of the latest mega-hotel casino's of Las Vegas – the Paris, the Bellagio and the Mandalay Bay – all demonstrating theming and replicature at a mega scale. Within this context of mega-resorts, however, is a 'haven' of a hotel that acts as a real hotel in the traditional sense – the Four Seasons Las Vegas.

With their international speciality in slick Classicism, the Four Seasons found a gap in the Vegas hotel market – the need for a sophisticated hotel with classical designs and no casino attached. Housing themselves in the top five floors of the existing Manadalay Bay Hotel, the Four Seasons offers a slice of luxury with conservative discretion, found no where else in Vegas. The design rationale for this hotel is elaborated in the introduction (see Talks: 'Designing Classicism in Vegas').

PARIS HOTEL AND CASINO, Las Vegas

Interior designer for public spaces: YATES–SILVERMAN INC, LAS VEGAS

Interior designer for rooms and suites: KOVACS & ASSOCIATES

1999   3000+ rooms   34 floors

'to bring the spirit, excitement and *savoir faire* of Paris to Vegas'

Since 1995 design teams from Park Place Entertainment have made numerous trips to Paris, France, to capture details of the city to transport to Vegas. The aim was to recreate the city of Paris, the city that has a special place in people's hearts, and bring to Vegas the Paris they remember or have always envisioned.

And so, from its French decor to its gaming, tables, its entertainments and famous landmark replicas down to its fine service and dining, and at a cost of $780 million, Paris Las Vegas likes to capture a slice of the great city of Paris.

This 3000 room hotel features a 50 storey high (540 ft) replica of the Eiffel Tower, façades of the Paris Opera House and Louvre, and a replica Arc de Triomphe around which the taxis drop off and pick up. Modelled after the Hotel de Ville, the hotel tower reaches some 34 storeys with their 2916 rooms and 295 suites.

Vegas's Eiffel Tower was built from the original drawings of Gustav Eiffel obtained from the Paris city authorities and the lighting designed to meet the specifications for the lighting that was added to the original tower for the 100th anniversary in 1989. Of its four, three of the tower's legs rise from inside the casino, breaking through the blue skies of the ceiling.

Unlike the original, the Eiffel Tower Las Vegas is fireproof and stable enough to withstand earthquakes.

Rooms are designed with 'rich French tastes' in mind, using heavy fabrics and furnishings, rich carpet patterns and gold drapes. The interiors also seek to replicate with cobblestoned sidewalks, façades of town houses, wrought iron street lamps and the Metro stand. It is more like a film set than a hotel.

The casino is surrounded by street scenes of Paris modelled after the Rue de la Paix with a ceiling painted to simulate the Parisian blue skies with their occasional cloud. The floor is cobblestoned, with ornate street signs directing to hotel, shops, ballroom or bathrooms. It is a place where time stands still, there are no clocks and no windows.

The check-in desks are able to turn around more people than an airport terminal. The space, lights and floor are ornate and lavish, and the desks are designed to divide guest from staff (or 'Citizens' as they are called) by a small iron gate.

Information boothes modelled from Parisian Metro stands act as LCD displays with game information.

Bar-in-the-round with video screen and under a blue cloudy sky.

This great hall is enclosed by walls of typical Parisian house fronts. The façades have been constructed above the check-in hall, casino, cafés and shops, and cover all parts of the wall with lit windows and coloured curtains. The shape of the great hall is not obvious; it is neither round nor square but curves and elongates in places reaching to corridors of shops with cobbled streets and free-standing wrought iron Parisian style street lamps. The restuarant and cafés are Disneyesque with fake moss growing up fake walls, with a fake town-bell in the middle of the buffet seating. However, the game is never too far away – Keno boards are everywhere with the latest selection of lucky numbers.

The round elevator lobby that has four sets of elevators to reach the 34 different floors is tastefully decorated with gold leaf and more delicate patterned motifs. Wrought iron and frosted glass awnings hang over each corridor.

The great hall which defines the gaming/lobby space of the Paris hotel is permanently set to a dim sort of light equivalent to Paris twilight. The ceiling, which is painted a sky blue with an occasional cloud, is pierced with three of the mighty legs of the Eiffel Tower poking through and interrupting the rows of the 2000 slot machines. It is an incredible sight. The shop that sells the merchandise for the Tower and tickets for the ride up there is located in one of the Tower's legs, perhaps to give the sales more authenticity.

The shopping mall features a wonderful coloured glass dome in the style of the Galerie Lafayette with swirly Art Deco type mosaic floor designs.

Rooms are designed with 'rich French tastes' in mind, using heavy fabrics and furnishings, rich carpet patterns and gold drapes. Bathrooms are spacious and lavish, and even the WC is given a lavish treatment.

BELLAGIO HOTEL AND CASINO, Las Vegas

Interior design led by ROGER THOMAS FOR MIRAGE RESORTS, LAS VEGAS

3000+ rooms   40+ floors   1998

'Italian make-believe in the heart of Vegas'

The $1.8 billion Bellagio, the most costly hotel/casino on Vegas' strip to date, is owned by Mirage Resorts – the name most associated with the transformation of Vegas beyond gambling into a world renowned hotel-resort destination. Their first mega-hotel/casino was The Mirage, which pioneered the way for theming in Vegas in 1989. Next came the Treasure Island Hotel which opened in 1993 with all the thrills and excitement of spectacular shows and make-believe.

The Mediterranean inspired Bellagio followed in 1998, appealing to a more sophisticated clientele with its excessive Italian flavour and distinctively European touch. Not only a flower-filled hotel, the Bellagio boasts a number of high class restaurants designed by names more associated with the East Coast; the Osteria del Circo restaurant was designed by Adam Tihany with views over Bellagio's own lake, and the Picasso restaurant hosts a remarkable collection of original Picasso masterpieces and a large collection of Picasso's ceramics.

The real jewel in the crown of the hotel's sales pitch, however, is 'the centrepiece of culture and refinement' – the Bellagio Gallery of Fine Art, which includes masterpieces mostly from the great European artists of the 18th, 19th and 20th centuries.

The company's aim was to supply something that was lacking locally – a connection with history that predates the city of Vegas. 'A spiritual heliport to the past, the Bellagio Gallery of Fine Art quietly changes everything in the cultural atmosphere of a place that henceforth will no longer be only spectacular and only new . . .' so goes the press release.

Roger Thomas, Design Director for Mirage Resorts, Las Vegas, talks about the design and the idea of replicature in the Bellagio hotel: 'The interior spaces of the Bellagio hotel are about intimate grandeur combined with a classic simplicity that allows you to feel calm and settled. These timeless designs inspired from Italy are able to be warm and grand at the same time. We try for a residential rather than a commercial attitude. The VIP lobby, for example, is more like a living room of a grand villa with fragile furnishings and soft colourings.

'We are not into "replicature" – where architecture tries to replicate. The idea of converting a beautiful old villa into a hotel like the Villa D'Este at Lake Como in Italy, is what we have modelled the Bellagio on. And this is why we have used real brass, real marble, and real gold leaf so we can achieve designs that are more realistic. However, the scale needs to be big enough to take your breath away but with details in human proportions so it may touch your sensibility.

'The small references may not be fully understood by all our clients, perhaps they are more "subliminal" but whether they are understood or not, I think it gives a richness of texture that people go home with. I think we now play to a more sophisticated audience who want romance and elegance.'

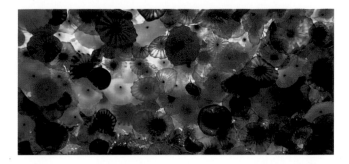

The reception desk overlooks a courtyard, arched and landscaped in the middle. The plaster of the inner walls is deliberately distressed or 'rubbed'. The space is dominated by a huge glass sculpture of over-sized glass flowers that hang above the centre of the lobby, consisting of over 2000 different coloured and sized glass petals that protrude from the ceiling.

The Conservatory garden is full of floral displays that are updated seasonally and theatrically lit, within which is the grand staircase leading to spa and gym, of the sort found in the grand villas of the 19th century. The mosaic floor is made of more than one million hand cut pieces of 30 different types of marble.

Even the shopping arcade is overflowing with Italianate designs

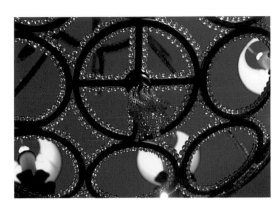

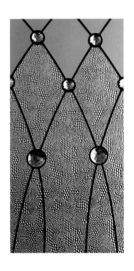

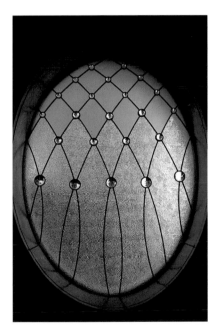

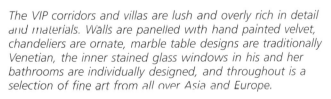

The VIP corridors and villas are lush and overly rich in detail and materials. Walls are panelled with hand painted velvet, chandeliers are ornate, marble table designs are traditionally Venetian, the inner stained glass windows in his and her bathrooms are individually designed, and throughout is a selection of fine art from all over Asia and Europe.

The Picasso restaurant hosts a remarkable collection of original Picasso masterpieces and a large collection of Picasso's ceramics set off by a colourful swirly carpet and a ceiling of pots.

'The centrepiece of culture and refinement' – the Bellagio Gallery of Fine Art, which includes masterpieces mostly from the great European artists of the 18th, 19th and 20th centuries.

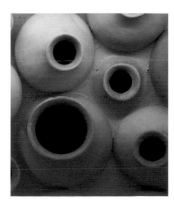

MANDALAY BAY HOTEL AND CASINO, Las Vegas

Interior designs: AVERY BROOKS & ASSOCIATES,

LAS VEGAS

1999   3700 rooms (500 suites)   41 floors

'contemporary with a tropical Vegas theme'

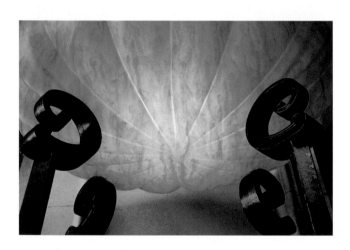

Featuring tropical themes with a mystical architecture and lush oriental surrounds, Mandalay Bay is one of the 'mega' hotels that opened early 1999 at a cost of $950 million and offers 3700 rooms including 500 suites. Room designs are considered contemporary with a tropical theme: chairs, for example, may be covered in leopard spot fabric, sitting up against mahogany wood tables.

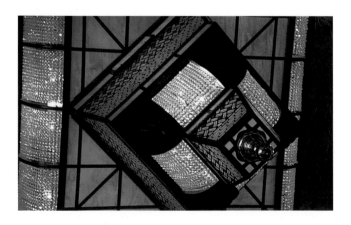

The lobby with its 35 check-in windows is dominated by huge oriental enclosed chandeliers and a 14ft tall aquarium containing 12 200 gallons of sea water and tropical fish.

The Coral Reef lounge in the gaming zone also offers aquatic views in its centre piece. The casino offers 122 gaming tables and 2400 slot machines taking up 135 000 sq ft.

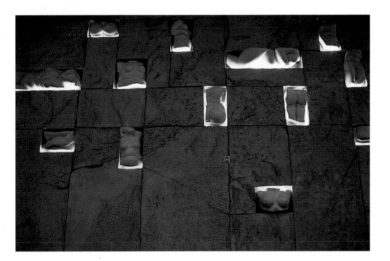

The mall, the retail centre piece, is still
expanding and will be dubbed the 'Mandalay
Mile' when it reaches its goal of stretching one
mile around. It is a mixture of hip restaurants,
groovy night-spots, regular shopping and a
wonderful array of contemporary art and light
installations.

The hotel has some fifteen restaurants including the Rum Jungle and in particular the Aureole. Designed by Adam Tihany it features an internationally renowned 42 ft high four storey 'wine tower' (where wine stewards are strapped onto harnesses and hoisted up the tower to make their selections) made of stainless steel and laminated glass where thousands of bottles are kept at perfect climatic conditions.

FOUR SEASONS HOTEL, Las Vegas

Interior design: AVERY BROOKS & ASSOCIATES, LAS VEGAS

1999   over 420 rooms (86 suites)   on the top five floors of the 46-storey building housing the Mandalay Bay Hotel

'breaking the mould of Vegas with a luxurious residence'

'We are the grand residence of Vegas,' says Charles Gruwell, Design Director of Avery Brooks & Associates, 'breaking the mould of Vegas designs on purpose. Instead of the high rise towers of glass and steel that characterise the Strip, we offer a luxury residential hotel in comparison.'

The Four Seasons Hotel in Las Vegas, which opened in March 1999, is the ultimate in discreet luxury in this electric city. A small 'boutique' hotel by Vegas standards that is uniquely located inside another hotel, it is also the first 'non-gaming' hotel in Vegas.

With just over 420 rooms including 86 suites but no casino, the Four Seasons boasts delicate attention to detail carried through all spaces, from materials used to the classical lines referred to. It occupies the five top floors of the Mandalay Bay Hotel, in consequence offering stunning views of both the Nevada Desert and the Las Vegas Strip from top to bottom.

Clean lines and fine art dominate the check-in desk.

The corridors and the lobby are spacious and uncluttered leaving room for appreciation of classic lines and exquisite materials. Discreet and gracious objets d'art are used as focal points in their own right, with hints of both ancient Far East and modern contemporary. Lighting is subdued throughout. Colour themes throughout are essentially natural with shades of honey, gold, green, amber and aubergine. Woods are warm with pecan and pear tones, marble is cool and with some selections in yellow.

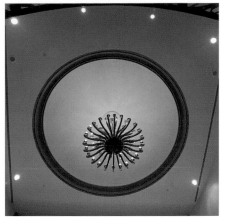

Over the hotel's grand sweeping staircase is an eye catching 17th century Italian cartoon on oilcloth by Renaissance artist Giuseppe Bezzuoli. Marble floors, brass balustrades and handles, and an opulent chandelier all add to the classical elegant flavour.

*Suites and bedrooms comprise eclectic
collections of furniture.*

The restaurant and entrance are detailed
with delicate textiles on comfortable sofas,
patterned iron doors, chequerboard and
spotted carpets, sweeping iron wall lights
and fine art.

contemporary resorts

In contrast to design by replicature found in the mega resort of Las Vegas, there are other resorts that are taking the marketability of good design more seriously. While remaining primarily a holiday destination, guests may also be impressed, if not lured, by staying in a contemporary designed hotel by a named designer.

This chapter presents just one stand-alone resort of El Gouna on Egypt's Red Sea coast, whose development company – Orascom – had the foresight to encourage new contemporary designs to attract a young clientele. They chose architect and designer Michael Graves to mix the indigenous with his own post-modern designs creating a fantastically unique hotel that has become a reference point within the local hotel design industry.

SHERATON MIRAMAR, El Gouna, Egypt

Interior design: MICHAEL GRAVES ARCHITECTS

1998   284 rooms   3 floors spread over a series of islands and lagoons.

'a unique experience of post-modern Graves on Egypt's Red Sea coast'

The Sheraton Miramar, which opened Spring 1998, is the first completed hotel project of three by Michael Graves Architects for this site. The hotel is designed as a series of shaped islands and themed clusters that are connected by wooden bridges across artificial lagoons, accommodating 284 rooms and suites.

Taking as source the Kafr El Gouna (the village centre) that was designed to typify Egyptian rural vernacular architecture, Graves was asked by the client to use these dome and vault forms as the point of departure for design. The most clear example of this homage to the vernacular are perhaps the guestroom domes which have remained in raw brick, the bed positioned directly underneath affording a 'raw' awakening for guests.

In his derivations from the local vocabulary Graves has successfully combined the indigenous with his geometrical elevations and decorations, resulting in a busy and lively exterior and a rich interior architecture full of surprises.

This 'rustic' assortment of tables, chairs and lights found throughout the hotel makes reference not only to local form but also to local manufacturing possibilities. As the Graves team discovered during the production phase,

adaptation rather than precision is the outcome, giving a more 'crude' line of furniture than originally designed.

Throughout the public spaces hang great chandeliers suspended from domes and hanging sequences of colourful glass or decorated metal lanterns. True to the traditions of Egyptian lighting found in the old and great palaces are the loose strings of metal chains that connect the otherwise invisible planes of domes. Fascinated by the traditional lighting used in other site projects Graves felt that their character was appropriate for some of the public areas and so invited the local lighting designer to design for these spaces.

Entering the lobby there is an expansive sense of light and space gathering focus under the luminescence of the great blue dome. With light streaming in from all sides the soft blues and yellows subdue the tone, and combined with the peaceful trickling of the water from the Roman fountain it is altogether a very relaxing initiation into the hotel.

Graves explains: 'We chose colours that from the day they were painted would, from the intense exposure to the sun, fade from the original bright colour to faded colours. We think that the stucco surfaces when rendered in this way take on a patina that links them more closely with their climate.'

Directly in front of the lobby is a small 'sheesha' terrace (otherwise known as the 'hubbly bubbly pipes' smoked throughout the Arab world) with small water fountains between each table. The terraces of the bar and restaurant are coloured with biscuit browns, blue domes and chains of small metal Islamic lights.

Interiors of rooms remain more simple using an almost ivory coloured stucco that serves to enhance the raw red brick of the dome while the 'Japanese' bathrooms are tiled in a deep blue. The lighting for the bare domes and vaults of the bedrooms, in contrast, takes on a deliberate modern style, clearly distinguishing from the traditional. 'I thought it was important to be explicit about the lights that were seen as our design and therefore modern. The lights for the guestrooms were designed to illuminate the vaults and domes that were minimal in character,' and in so doing juxtapose the old with the new.

Behind the doors of the more upmarket Executive and Presidential Suites, however, pinks can be found wrapping blues, yellows framing pinks, and ivories comforting yellows. Furniture is simple but rustic.

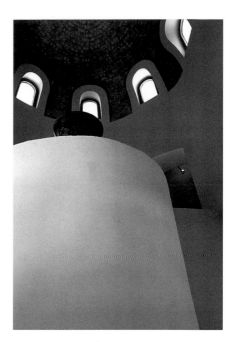

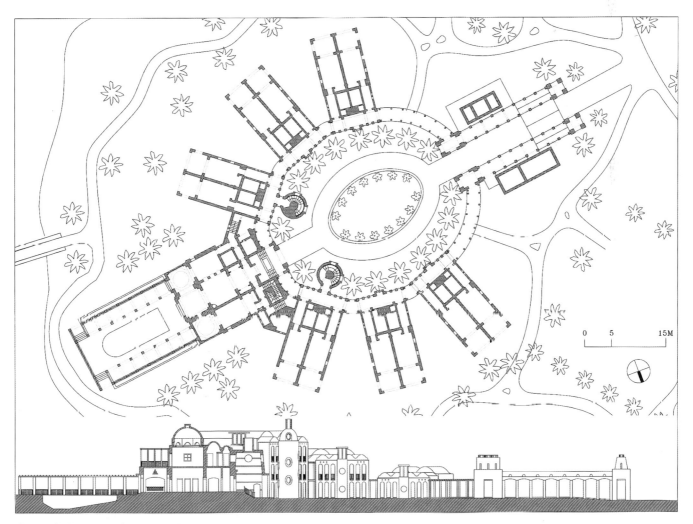

Plan and elevation of the Presidential suite.

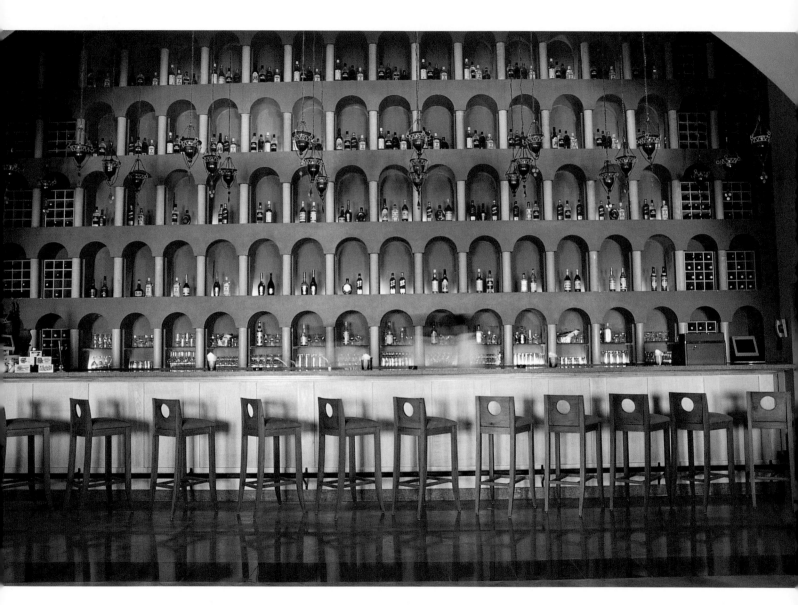

The impressively tall bar area is brought into context with the series of turquoise blue glass lights hung in regular formation and wrapped with metal chains with dangling tassels.

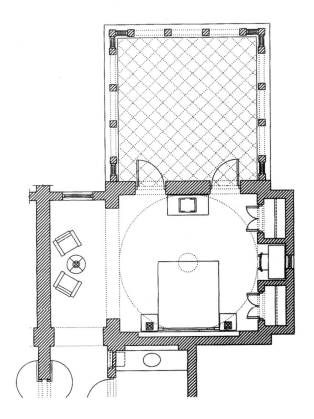

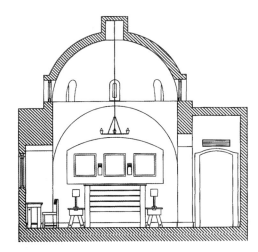

Plan of a bedroom and section of a suite.

Another small but delightful detail is found in the textiles used for the bar's armchairs that weave golden Pharonic stars into cloth.

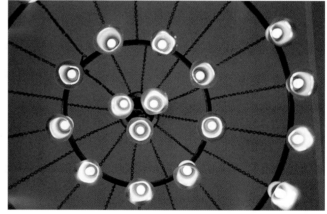

The restaurant is a grand spectacle of striped vaults leading to the 'buffet-in-the-round' at the far end with its decorative floor. The blue striped vaults make explicit reference to the tent, a structure used throughout Egypt's deserts by the Bedouin tribes; says Graves, 'I have always loved the kind of light that comes through the canvas of tents, especially while dining.'

Outdoor staircase connecting levels. The Graves team hope that guests will be able to identify with the shapes, colours and details rather than just have another 'international' hotel experience.

The wave theme washes into the canopy of the main and oriental restaurant terraces interweaving course hesian through blue, and into the rippling handrails of guestroom balconies.

atrium

Working in vast spaces that are so well defined architecturally, it is a challenge for the interior designer to find his own theme and identity. It becomes his task to soften textures in the context of hard industrial materials, to enclose spaces in the context of high open rooms, and to give a more human scale to the tall high-tech structures so that the hotel guest can recognise himself within the space.

Some solutions involve the extensive use of fine art and sculpture, in the case of the Shinjuku Park Tower; and the use of mixed materials, both hard and soft, natural and manufactured. In contrast, Graves' interiors for the Hyatt Regency Fukuoka create an even greater sense of the 'grand' in the public spaces, by emphasising the rotunda through colour and the temple through gold leaf. Intimacy and human scale is kept to the rooms only.

The two airport hotel projects present a slightly different challenge where the designer must harmonise his designs within the context of fantastic airport architecture and its transient guest. In the case of the Hyatt Regency Paris, Hirsch Bedner Associates have used the natural leaves of the garden and light textiles to soften the hard edge of the aluminium structure. Whereas for the Sheraton Paris Roissy, ECART have been faced with a hotel that is actually in the airport itself. In contrast to the other design solutions, ECART have lent their designs to the futuristic structure with sleek contemporary lines and palettes interrupted only by the warmth of the wood based furniture.

PARK HYATT, West Shinjuku, Tokyo

Interior architecture: KENZO TANGE

Interior design: JOHN MORFORD
1994   178 rooms   occupies top 14 floors of a 52-storey skyscraper

'bold soaring architecture combined with thrilling interiors'

A luxury hotel that crowns the 52-storey Shinjuku Park Tower, it is a feast of modern interior design and architecture, fine art and sculpture, and panoramic views all the way to Mount Fuji. Architect Kenzo Tange designed the massive honed granite and glass sculptured building, in which Hong Kong based interior designer John Morford worked many surprises in his modern contemporary style. Steel, glass, wood, geometry and Zen combine to create this modernist decor high above the city.

The Tower comprises three connecting towers each crowned by a soaring, glass enclosed space that has been adapted as the key feature of the hotel – the atrium affording a great sense of sky and space in the four storey glass pyramid.

Morford works with the exterior in his use of granite and glass on the inside. In contrast, the use of wood is warming, and wallcovers of natural fibre and wool carpets serve to soften the overall spaces. Morford commissioned artists and sculptors from all over the world to create a unique collection for the hotel.

The Tower comprises three connecting towers each crowned by a soaring, glass enclosed space that has been adapted as the key feature of the hotel – the atrium, with lounge and adjoining bar.

Morford works with the exterior in his use of granite and glass on the inside in the lounge and library. In contrast, the use of wood is warming, and wallcovers of natural fibre and wool carpets serve to soften the overall spaces. The library has an impressive selection of over 2000 books, CD and laser discs.

The rooms (on floors 42 through to 51) are large at 50sq metres for a standard room, the largest in Tokyo and with a natural colour palette act as a serene retreat and efficient private office for the business traveller. Walls are panelled with a rare water elm from northern Japan whose grain is rich and warm. Oversized marble and granite bathrooms boast an extra deep tub and oil paintings by Yoshitaka Echizenya.

Covering the walls of the restaurant Girandole are Vera Mercer's four immense montages of 144 faces captured on black and white film in European cafes.

The Japanese restaurant Kozue, boasts views of Mount Fuji from its tiered seating and is finished with a more natural colour palette. Two towers made of bamboo represent traditional craft and the modern.

The hotel also houses one of the most chic and stylish health clubs. Here the pool in the glass pyramid.

The 52nd floor houses the New York Bar and Grill designed to capture the vibrancy of the Big Apple with a monochrome palette and four huge vibrant paintings of New York by Italian artist Valerio Adami.

SHERATON PARIS AIRPORT, Roissy

Architecture: PAUL ANDREU/MARTINET ARCHITECTURE

Interior design: ECART
1996   265 rooms   5 floors

From the plane to the room, located inside Terminal 2 of Paris' Charles de Gaulle Airport and housed inside a futurist architecture are the clean contemporary designs of ECART – the design studio that started the trend in 'boutique' hotel interiors in 1984 with Morgans, New York (then led by design name Andrée Putman).

From the glazed central atrium with the four glass galleried storeys that look in, it becomes a world of glass. Floor, balustrades, roof, all made either in part or entirely of glass or polished surfaces reflect different perspectives on and into the space.

A tidy central back-lit panelled service 'bubble' running nearly the length of the foyer hides entrances, lifts and services.

Materials and colours are deliberately warming set against this cool sharp dramatic backdrop – oak doors, cherrywood and sand coloured furniture, marbled bathrooms.

Simple, sleek, no-fuss designs for a hotel that caters largely to the needs of transient business guests, with 16 spaces functioning as meeting/seminar rooms.

The impressive spectacle of glass, light and reflections in the glass atrium and its galleries. Corridors retain clean and simple lines with a light palette and star wall lights.

In contrast to the atrium's world of glass, the check-in desk warms with its dark woods and polished floors.

The central service 'bubble' that tidies up the service and entrance areas in a back-lit glass panelled house.

Business areas are sleek and functional. Colours are predominantly blue, beige and grey, surfaces polished and clean.

Blues, browns, glass and space, are themes that run throughout the other public areas of the bar and restaurant.

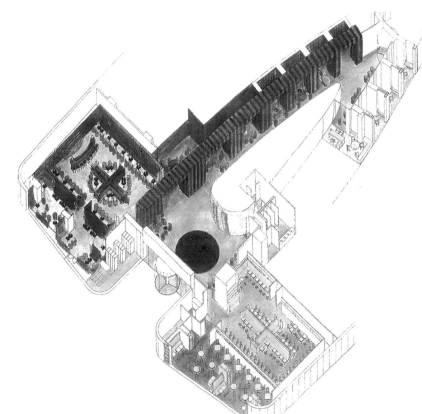

Ground floor plan.

HYATT REGENCY, Roissy, Paris

Architecture: MURPHY/JAHN

Interior design: HIRSCH BEDNER ASSOCIATES
1992   400 rooms   Two 5 floor blocks   Atrium lobby

Architecturally, the glass and steel Hyatt Regency Roissy is a modern interpretation of the Parisian courtyard hotel, playing on the interrelationship between interior and exterior gardens and rooms, with an aluminium skin and curving roof geometry. The hotel's central axis is defined by two five-storey hotel room blocks, which form the spatial edges for the exterior courtyard garden and the interior atrium garden.

The interior garden atrium and the exterior garden court create the central focus for the hotel providing a space to move in and out of as well as to relax in.

Keeping to the framework of the architecture, while renovating the Apollo restaurant – itself an 'oval' within the atrium lobby – HBA added elements to this metal and timber defined area. To make the space feel more relaxing and inviting these were applied to the oval above and the boundary of the oval walls.

Fabric was also introduced in contrast to the solid metals, in a white basket weave, to give more privacy. Working with existing black granite and light wood they added textual wall covering in the buffet seating area, again to soften the overall feel of the space. Outside the oval additional 'outdoor' seats were added covered in the same white fabric giving a sense of enclosure to the high space of the lobby.

The white fabric, as a theme, also runs through the Cosmos Bar. In an attempt to overcome the challenge of intimate lighting in a space which reaches five storeys high, HBA designed a canopy at the bar that was back-lit and added small lamps to the lounge tables. A colourful carpet was also added to soften the area. Furniture was re-upholstered in textural fabrics and crafted from rich mahogany woods.

Rooms were given the same treatment as the restaurant – bringing a light colour palette with coloured jewel tone fabrics. Stark industrial furnishings were replaced with sleek, simplified profiles with a comfortable residential feel.

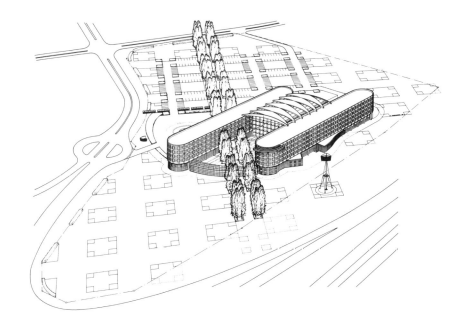

View and sketch of the exterior showing the huge glass and steel structure and its two five storey hotel room blocks, which form the spatial edges for the exterior courtyard garden and the interior atrium garden.

High view of the central atrium lobby, restaurant and seating area (before HBA's interior additions).

The Apollo restaurant in the centre of the lobby, softened and enclosed through the use of white fabric, above and around.

Check in desk and lobby softened by the use of colourful carpets.

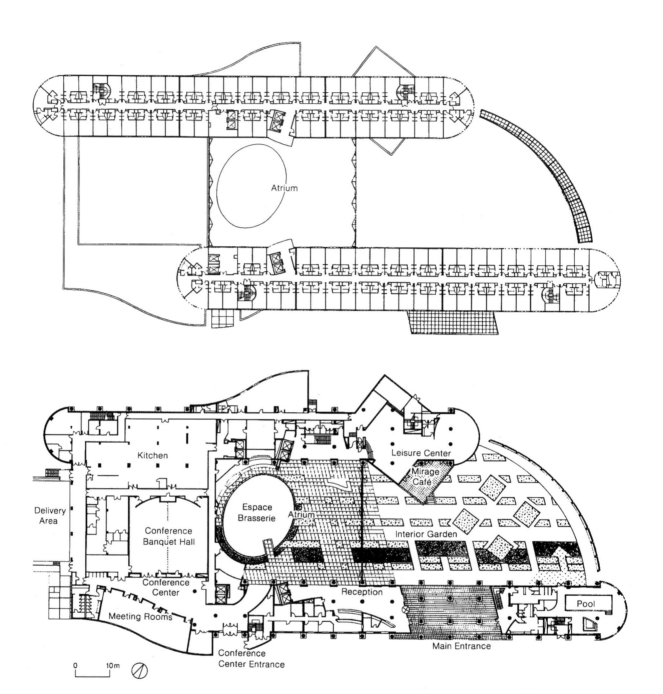

Atrium

Kitchen

Leisure Center

Mirage Café

Delivery
Area

Espace
Brasserie

Atrium

Interior Garden

Conference
Banquet Hall

Conference
Center

Reception

Pool

Meeting Rooms

0   10m

Conference
Center Entrance

Main Entrance

Floor plan and section.

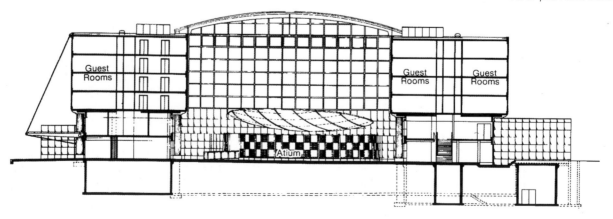

Guest
Rooms

Guest
Rooms

Guest
Rooms

Atrium

HBA designed a canopy at the bar that was back-lit to bring a more intimate feel to the space.

Rooms were given the same treatment as the restaurant – bringing a light colour palette with coloured jewel tone fabrics. Stark industrial furnishings were replaced with sleek, simplified profiles with a comfortable residential feel.

FUKUOKA HYATT REGENCY

Architecture and interior design: MICHAEL GRAVES

1993 260 rooms 13 storey rotunda

'grand and attractive functional mix of business and hotel'

This business-oriented hotel comprises a 13 storey rotunda with two six-storey wings which form an entrance court facing a park. This building is in fact part of a larger complex that is organised in three distinct parts: an office block, hotel and hotel ballroom (a one-storey pavilion at the rear of the office block).

The rotunda is made from copper clad columns supported by a red sandstone base; the six-storey wings are clad in limestone and granite.

Inside, an atrium extending the length of the building provides natural light into the adjacent spaces which would otherwise be in the dark due to the configuration of the site. The hotel lobby in the centre of the rotunda is lit from above by a dramatic pyramidal structure which can be viewed from the guestroom corridor in the rotunda.

At the entrance to the office building atrium, a gold-leafed 'temple' serves as a grand stair, connecting the several public areas of the hotel. This 'temple' works as a dramatic focal point and is used extensivley for grand celebrations.

The interior decoration, also by Graves, allows his very distinctive geometric design signature to be carried all the way from the exterior through the public spaces to the rooms.

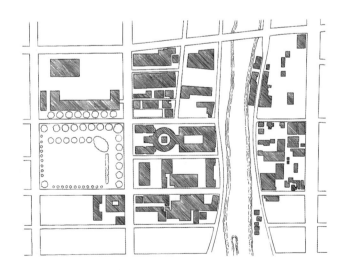

Site plan and exterior view of the hotel rotunda, made from copper clad columns supported by a red sandstone base; the six-storey wings are clad in limestone and granite.

Section.

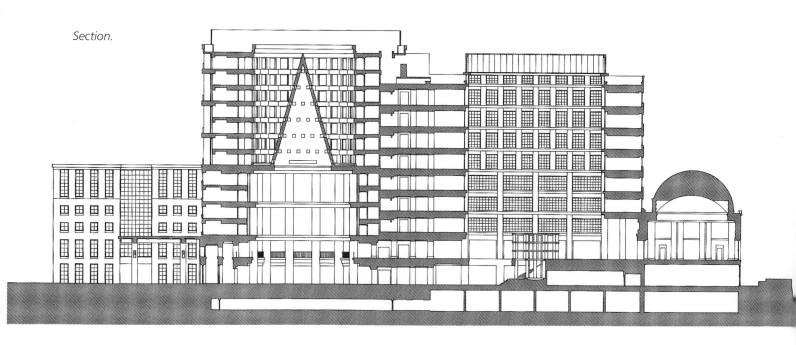

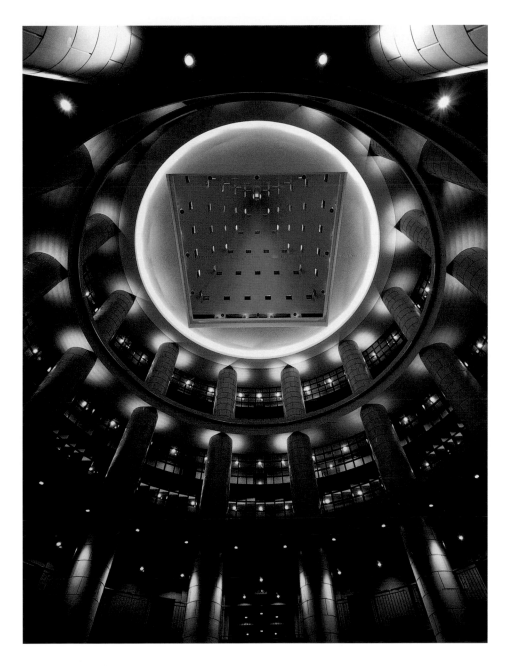

Inside the hotel rotunda, an atrium extending the length of the building provides natural light into the adjacent spaces which would otherwise be in the dark due to the configuration of the site. The rotunda is topped with a pyramid-shaped hat that is punctuated with skylights.

The hotel lobby in the centre of the rotunda is lit from above by a dramatic pyramidal copper structure which can be viewed from the guestroom corridor in the rotunda.

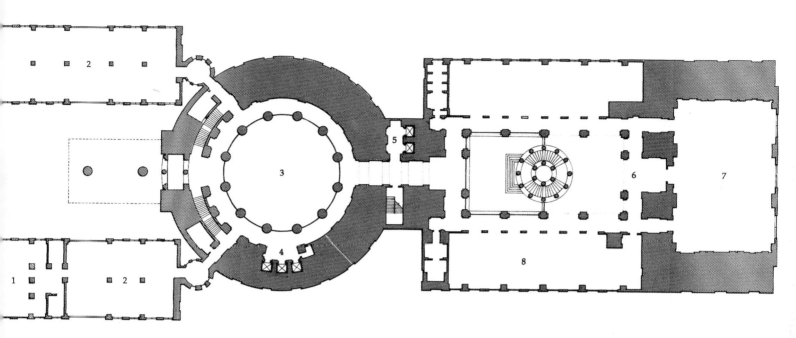

Second floor plan.

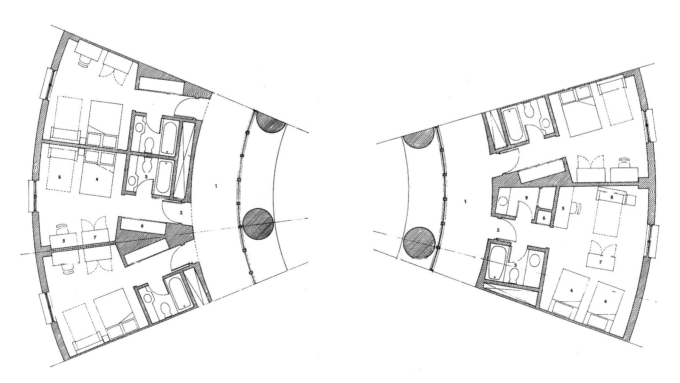

Plans of room layout as organised around the rotunda.

Groundfloor seating looking through the Rotunda.

The mini golden rotunda that as well as acting as the entrance to the office building, serves as a golden 'temple' and is used frequently for wedding celebrations.

Rooms are tidy and simply furnished, with a calming colour palette. They are set up in such a way as to sleep a maximum number of people in beds that fold down and on convertible couches that pull out. Furniture is custom made by Graves, with his usual play on geometry found in the chair-backs, table-legs and lamp stands.

new classics

The boldness in the way the architecture and interiors make reference to classical design in the two projects presented in this last chapter is so clear as to warrant the label 'new classics'. Though potentially loaded with the weight of the Savoys and Ritzs of the world, these two projects rather carry classical design elements on the back of a subtle and sophisticated use of modern design trends.

Lines are sleek, not interrupted; fabrics are sumptuous, not tassled and fringed; spaces are fresh, not busy. The 'ornamental' elements of what we usually think of as classical are gone and in their place are explicit references to periods of design such as Art Deco and Art Nouveau, manifested in new materials, soft colours and grand spaces.

The New Classic also targets the business and leisure audience by offering the highest standards for both. Quality of materials and finishings is unrelentingly consistent throughout, and the overall result is a solid work of contemporary design that is likely to stand the test of time.

FOUR SEASONS, New York City

Interior design: CHAADA SIEMBIEDA REMEDIOS INC.
1993   370 rooms   52 floors

**'The graceful limestone spire soars above the quintessential Manhattan address.
A sleek monument to New York sophistication'**

The Four Seasons New York City has a dynamic vertical exterior with soothing, contemporary, minimalist interiors, that soften and complement the structural heights and large volumes. It opened in June 1993 in central Manhattan, between Park and Madison Avenues, and at 682 feet is the tallest hotel in New York City. (At least half the guest rooms have views over Central Park.)

The 52 floor hotel with 370 rooms occupies the entire depth between 57th and 58th Streets and is an elegant play on 1920s and 1930s Art Deco and Art Nouveau classics. Fabrics, finishes and colours have been selected to fit the neutral honey tones, soft greys and beiges of the English sycamore, limestone and marble. The finest silks, wool, leathers, wood and metals are used in soft shades of grey, bronze, celadon, caramel, green and cognac.

A French limestone base with oversized windows rises four storeys flush with the pavement, followed by seven graduated steps into a skyscraper tower capped by the 3000 sq ft Presidential Suite on the top floor. With each step, the number of rooms per floor decreases while the number of suites increases. Exterior and interior walls are clad in a honey coloured French Magny limestone.

The grand lobby, from 57th Street, terraced and three storeys high is a wonderfully impressive entrance with an almost Pharonic temple-like vastness to it. The foyer with 33 ft high back-lit onyx ceiling set on huge columns, and with a patterned marble floor, unfolds a sequence of raised lobby-lounges on either side, which in turn lead to the dining areas that face on to 58th Street. The hotel's artwork, displayed throughout the public spaces, features signed prints by Le Corbusier, Mariani, Magritte and Kandinsky.

Light panel detail beneath the fabric panelled wall in the lobby lounge.

Between the bar and the Fifty Seven Fifty Seven restaurant is featured a large glazed circular window framed in beech.

A variation on the classic brasserie. The restaurant Fifty Seven Fifty Seven and bar feature 22 ft high coffered ceilings, maple floors, walnut inlays, and bronze chandeliers with onyx inlays. With chairs by Dakota Jackson and art by early 20th century French artist Kimon Nicolaides, it features the 1935 Manhattan Merry-Go-Round, a lively charcoal sketch depicting people from all walks of life parading around a merry-go-round. Images of this adorn the walls and the finished piece has been enlarged and etched on a mirror that reflects the room from above the bar.

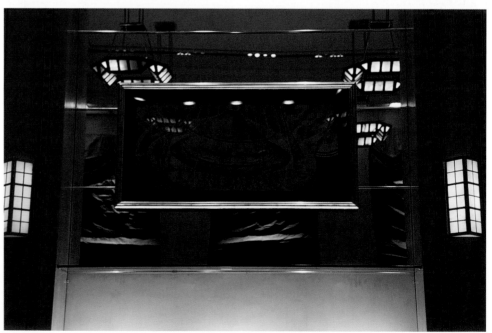

Staircases are wide with glass panelling, framed by tall frosted glass bronze lanterns. English sycamore is used throughout public areas and rooms giving a very soft honey tone to all surfaces.

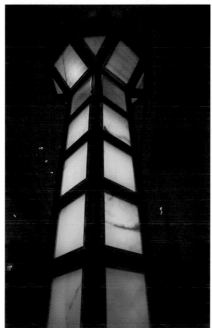

The pattern of the large glazed circular window is reflected in the three 14 ft high hand crafted Italian Scagliola panels which hang in the Fifty Seven Fifty Seven restaurant. Sofas are sumptuously covered with Art Deco chequered black and sliver ribbed velvet.

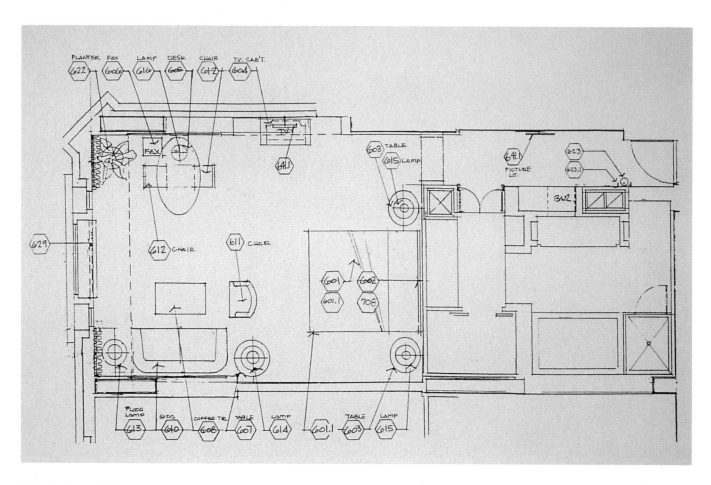

PLANTER FAX LAMP DESK CHAIR TV. CAB'T.
622 606 616 605 617 604

603 TABLE
615 LAMP

641.1 PICTURE LT.

623
623.1

BAR

629

612 CHAIR   611 CHAIR

601
601.1   602
708

FLOOR LAMP   SOFA   COFFEE TR.   TABLE   LAMP   TABLE   LAMP
613   610   608   607   614   601.1 603   615

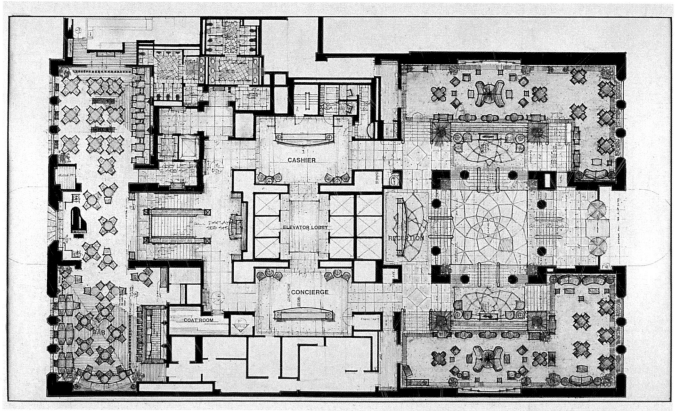

CASHIER

ELEVATOR LOBBY

RECEPTION

CONCIERGE

COAT ROOM

BAR

Bedroom plan and ground floor plan.

Guest rooms, spacious and individually designed, are dominated by use of English sycamore wood which has a unique grain and is very luscious. Colours are primarily caramel and light green. Each room features five pieces of exclusive art from the 1900s–1950s.

FOUR SEASONS CANARY WHARF, London

Interior design: UNITED DESIGNERS
1999   139 rooms   10 floors

'A modern classic . . . with a 21st century outlook'

Classical meets modern in this chic, sleek hotel that opened at the end of 1999, boasting excellent views over the River Thames and set in London's latest business community.

Its distinctive 10 storey facade features bold 'ice cube' windows and two, seven-storey high mahogany 'doors' dramatically frame the entrance.

The three-storey high lobby defines four areas either side of the central staircase, distinguishable as four timber lined 'cubes' – the theme throughout the interiors. These house the concierge's desk, the cloakroom, the lounge bar and the reception. The stairs themselves feature a finely etched silver reed balustrade that snakes upwards across clear glass; to the rear of the stairway is a rug carrying the 'cube' motif in colours blackcurrant and taupe.

The crisp light lobby uses a palette of cream tones enriched by blackcurrants and black walnut furniture. The hotel's Italian restaurant, in contrast, is warm and intimate with the kitchen exposed giving a panoramic view on to the chef's creations. The seating upholstery, lampshade and carpets also carry the cube motif.

Rooms demonstrate the mix of classical and modern materials in the use of cream leather in the window seat with the dark timber of the furnishings. Cream marble with alabaster glass wall tiles create a fresh bathroom set against to the rich black walnut furnishings.

Situated in the heart of London's more recent business centre, only 10 minutes from London's smaller City Airport, and in part of a mixed-use estate development of luxury apartments, health clubs and spa with large pool the hotel aims to be a magnet for both business and leisure travellers.

The 'ice cube' windows of the facade.

The main functions of the clean spacious lobby are oriented around the dominating staircase.

The restaurant introduces warm blackcurrants and softer wood furnishings.

Ground floor plan.

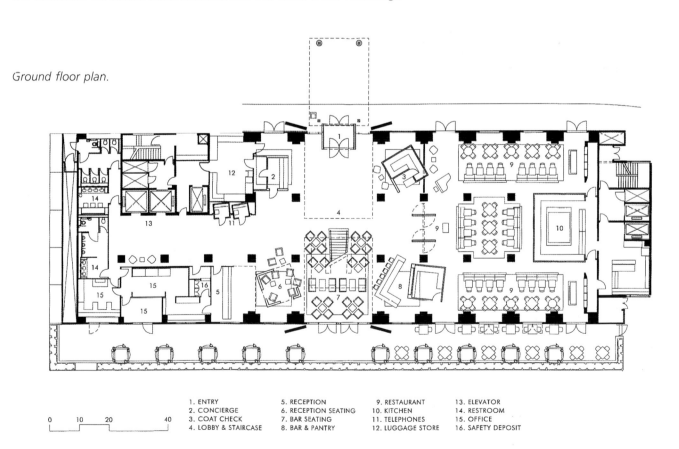

0   10   20   40

1. ENTRY	5. RECEPTION	9. RESTAURANT	13. ELEVATOR
2. CONCIERGE	6. RECEPTION SEATING	10. KITCHEN	14. RESTROOM
3. COAT CHECK	7. BAR SEATING	11. TELEPHONES	15. OFFICE
4. LOBBY & STAIRCASE	8. BAR & PANTRY	12. LUGGAGE STORE	16. SAFETY DEPOSIT

Cream marble and alabaster tiles freshen the bathrooms.

The rooms use a modern natural palette of creams and mushrooms but with classical lines and furnishings.

HOTEL LISTINGS

Bellagio Hotel and Casino, Las Vegas
36+ Las Vegas Blvd South
Las Vegas
Nevada 89109
USA
Tel: + 1 702 693 7147 (PR office)
Fax: + 1 702 693 8665

Delano
1685 Collins Avenue
Miami Beach
FL 33139
USA
Tel + 1 305 672 2000
Fax + 1 305 532 0099

Dwar El Omda
Kafr El Gouna
El Gouna Resort
near Hurghada
Red Sea
Egypt
Tel: + 20 65 545 060/2/3
Fax: + 20 65 545 061

Four Seasons Canary Wharf London
46 Westferry Circus
London E14
UK
Tel + 44 20 7 510 1999
ax + 44 20 7 510 1998

Four Seasons Hotel Istanbul
Tevkifhane Sokak No 1
34490 Sultanahmet-Eminönü
Istanbul
Turkey
Tel: + 90 212 638 8200
Fax: + 90 212 638 8210

Four Seasons Hotel Milano
Via Gesú 8
Milano 20121
Italy
Tel: + 39 02 77088
Fax: + 39 02 7708 5007

Four Seasons Las Vegas
3960 Las Vegas Boulevard South
Las Vegas
Nevada 89119
USA
Tel: + 1 702 632 5212
Fax: + 1 702 632 5222

Four Seasons New York
57 East 57th Street
New York
NY 10022
USA
Tel: + 1 212 758 5700
Fax: + 1 212 758 5711

Grand Hyatt Berlin
Marlene-Dietrech-Platz 2
D-10785 Berlin
Germany
Tel + 49 30 2553 1234
Fax + 49 30 2553 1235

Hotel Albergo
137 rue Abdel Wahab el-Inglizi
Beirut
Lebanon
Tel: + 961 1 33 97 97
Fax: + 961 1 33 99 99

Hotel Montalembert
3 Rue de Montalembert
75+7 Paris
France
Tel: + 33 1 45 49 68 68
Fax: + 33 1 45 49 69 49

Hotel Square
3 Rue de Boulainvilliers
75016 Paris
France
Tel : + 33 1 44 14 91 90
Fax: + 33 1 44 14 91 99

Hyatt Regency Fukouka
2-14-1 Hakataeki Higashi
Hakata-ku
Fukuoka 812-0013
Japan
Tel: + 81 9 2412 1234
Fax: + 81 9 2414 2490

Hyatt Regency Paris
Charles De Gaulle
351 Avenue du Bois de la Pie
BP 40048, Paris Nord II
95912 Roissy CDG
France
Tel: + 33 1 48 17 12 34
Fax: + 33 1 48 17 17 17

Le Méridien Lingotto
Via Nizza 262
Torino 10126
Italy
Tel: + 39 011 664 2000
Fax: + 39 011 664 2001

Mandalay Bay Hotel and Casino, Las Vegas
3950 Las Vegas Blvd South
Las Vegas
Nevada 89119
USA
Tel: +1 702 632 7700
Fax: +1 702 632 7705

Mondrian
8440 Sunset Boulevard
West Hollywood
Los Angeles CA 90069
USA
Tel: +1 323 650 8999
Fax: + 1 323 650 5215

Morgans
237 Madison Avenue
New York
NY 1+16
USA
Tel: + 1 212 686 0300
Fax: + 1 212 686 9401

One Aldwych
1 Aldwych
London WC2B 4BZ
UK
Tel:+ 44 0207 300 1000
Fax:+ 44 0207 300 1001

Paramount
235 West 46th Street
New York City
NY 1+36
USA
Tel: + 1 212 764 5500
Fax: + 1 2112 354 5237

Paris Hotel and Casino, Las Vegas
3655 Las Vegas Blvd South
Las Vegas
NV 89109 – 4343
USA
Tel: + 1 702 946 7000

Park Hyatt Tokyo
3-7-1-2- Nishi-Shinjuku
Shinjuku-ku
Tokyo 163-1055
Japan
Tel: + 81 3 5322 1234
Fax: + 81 3 5322 1288

Royalton
44 West 44th Street
New York City
NY1+36
USA
Tel: + 1 212 869 4400
Fax: + 1 212 869 8965

Sheraton Miramar
El Gouna Village
near Hurghada
Egypt
Tel: + 20 65 545606
Fax: + 20 65 545608

Sheraton Paris Airport
Aerogare Charles de Gaulle 2
BP 30051
95716 Roissy Aerogare
Paris
France
Tel: + 33 1 49 19 70 70
Fax: + 33 1 49 19 70 71

SoHo Grand Hotel
310 West Broadway
New York
NY 10013
USA
Tel: +1 212 965 3000
Fax: + 1 212 965 3200

St Martins Lane
45 St Martins Lane
London WC2N 4HX
UK
Tel: + 44 0207 300 5500
Fax: + 44 0207 300 5501

The Halkin Hotel
5 Halkin Street
Belgravia
London SW1X 7DJ
UK
Tel: + 44 0207 333 1000
Fax: + 44 0207 333 1100

The Mercer Hotel
147 Mercer Street
New York
NY 10012
USA
Tel: +1 212 966 6060
Fax: +1 212 965 3838

The Metropolitan
Old Park Lane
London W1Y 4LB
UK
Tel: + 44 0207 447 1000
Fax: + 44 0207 447 1100

The Morrison
Ormond Quay
Dublin
Ireland
Tel: + 353 1 887 2400
Fax: + 353 1 887 2499

The Standard
8300 Sunset Boulevard
Hollywood
CA 90069
USA
Tel: + 1 323 650 9090

W Atlanta
111 Perimeter Center West
Atlanta
GA 30346
USA
Tel: + 1 770 396 6800
Fax: + 1 770 394 4805

W New York
541 Lexington Avenue
New York
NY 10022
USA
Tel: + 1 212 407 2981
Fax: + 1 212 421 3876

W San Francisco
181 Third Street
San Francisco
CA 94103
USA
Tel: + 1 415 777 5300
Fax: + 1 415 817 7800

W Seattle
1112 Fourth Avenue
Seattle
WA 98101
USA
Tel: + 1 206 264 6000
Fax: + 1 206 264 6100
Fax: + 1 323 650 2820